Medical Ethics and Law
An introduction

Victoria Tippett

Senior House Officer
Accident and Emergency Department
Newham Hospital, London

Forewords
by
Richard Ashcroft
and
Raanan Gillon

Radcliffe Publishing
Oxford • San Francisco

Radcliffe Publishing Ltd
18 Marcham Road
Abingdon
Oxon OX14 1AA
United Kingdom

www.radcliffe-oxford.com
Electronic catalogue and worldwide online ordering facility.

_____

British Library Cataloguing in Publication Data

A catalogue record for this book is available from the British Library.

ISBN 1 85775 894 3

Typeset by Aarontype Ltd, Easton, Bristol
Printed and bound by TJ International Ltd, Padstow, Cornwall

Contents

Forewords   v

About the authors   ix

Acknowledgements   x

CHAPTER 1
Truthfulness, trust and good communication   1
Victoria Tippett

CHAPTER 2
Consent   9
Victoria Tippett

CHAPTER 3
Confidentiality   17
Victoria Tippett

CHAPTER 4
Children, medicine and law   27
Victoria Tippett and Thiraupathy Marianayagam

CHAPTER 5
Mental health   37
Victoria Tippett and Thiraupathy Marianayagam

CHAPTER 6
Life and death, dying and killing   47
Victoria Tippett

CHAPTER 7
Human reproduction   65
Victoria Tippett and Louise Ma

CHAPTER 8
The GMC, complaints and whistleblowing   81
Victoria Tippett and Louise Ma

CHAPTER 9
Medical research   95
Victoria Tippett

CHAPTER 10
Rationing and resources   111
Victoria Tippett

CHAPTER 11
Healthcare rights   121
Victoria Tippett

CHAPTER 12
The new genetics   129
Victoria Tippett

Resources   139
Cases   145
Statutes and bills   147
Appendix   149
Index   151

Foreword

The book you have in your hands is to help you understand the main ethical and legal details you need to know in order to practise medicine safely and well. It was written by three medical graduates of Imperial College, who had studied the intercalated degree in Healthcare Ethics and Law at Manchester University. The writing of the book was first put to me by Victoria Tippett, and she and her colleagues produced the book, working in their spare time, entirely under their own initiative, and with little active support from me. They are to be congratulated on producing something so well written and well informed, on their dedication and hard work in bringing the project to fruition, and on putting in so much effort to produce something useful and helpful to other students studying medicine.

Medical ethics and law have been a compulsory part of undergraduate medical education in the United Kingdom for only about 12 years, since the General Medical Council's report *Tomorrow's Doctors* was published. All UK medical schools now include some medical ethics teaching in their curricula, but it has taken some time for this to become fully established. So many students now close to graduating have not had much teaching on this important topic. This book is intended to help fill that gap.

Medical ethics is an inherently fascinating subject, and throws up new issues every day – just look at the newspapers or the *British Medical Journal*! But most of these issues are matters for specialist consideration; there are some topics which every new doctor should know about and understand, because they are a central part of your own medical practice, in most of your work with patients. Good ethical thinking requires practice and application. But ethics and law are central parts of your clinical knowledge and skill, and there are some essentials which you can grasp and learn quite quickly. This book should help you with that.

This book contains short summaries, with examples and guidance on your legal position, of a series of the core topics of medical ethics and law. The list of topics was defined in 1996, when a consensus conference of the teachers of medical ethics and law in UK medical schools, a broad group of doctors, nurses, chaplains, ethicists and lawyers, described a core curriculum for medical ethics.[1]

You can get further information about the topics covered in this book from a number of sources: the British Medical Association (BMA), the General Medical Council (GMC) (especially its Duties of a Doctor pamphlets), and the defence unions/societies. There are a number of good guides to law for doctors and to medical ethics. But the aim of this book is to give you some guides to effective, safe and good clinical practice. It is only the starting point: as you gain experience and skill in practising medicine, you will also gain knowledge and skill in the ethical aspects of the job. I wish you every success in this!

Richard Ashcroft
Reader in Biomedical Ethics
Imperial College Faculty of Medicine
August 2004

Reference

1   Ashcroft RE, Baron D, Benatar S *et al.* (1998) Teaching medical ethics and law within medical education: a model for the UK core curriculum. *J Med Ethics.* **24**: 188–92.

Foreword

What a delight to be invited to write one of the forewords to a book on medical ethics and law written by three young doctors. A delight for several reasons. First, because this book will be really helpful to medical students and newly qualified doctors in understanding their ethical and legal obligations in medical practice, and, dare one say it, also helpful to well-established doctors! Second, because page after page it demonstrates the centrality of medical ethics and law to medical practice (and thus, of course, its core relevance in medical education). Third, because it succinctly explains each component of the core curriculum for medical ethics and law in medical education that a multidisciplinary group comprised mostly of teachers of the subject devised in the 1990s. Fourth, because the book is written by *young* doctors who have such obvious enthusiasm for the subject as a practical aspect of their medical lives. It is upon young doctors and medical students that the future of medical practice depends and the caring yet thorough approach demonstrated in this book augurs well for that future. Finally, it is a delight to see medical students at Imperial College London – as these authors were when they first started working on this book for publication – once again producing student-led work in medical ethics. (A previous group produced a 'Declaration of a New Doctor' as a sort of contemporary version of the Hippocratic Oath to which the whole year committed themselves on graduating as doctors.) Not all medical schools have succeeded in inspiring their medical students so positively in this newish aspect of medical education, but the Medical Ethics Unit at Imperial College London and the Manchester University Centre for Social Ethics, where all of the authors took an intercalated degree in medical ethics and law before continuing their medical studies at Imperial, are among the medical schools that have.

Of course, there are aspects of the book that readers will disagree with – I do myself – but such contentiousness is characteristic of both ethics and (surprisingly) law and is to be expected. Readers will find themselves challenged by a variety of dilemmas, and guided through ethical and legal arguments presenting a variety of views, sometimes with clear advice about their legal and professional obligations, where these are clear, and sometimes with advice that there are conflicting legal and ethical opinions and on appropriate steps to take in such circumstances.

One word of caution. While the authors have clearly done an impressive amount of reading and research into medical law as well as medical ethics, they are not themselves lawyers, and financial constraints prevented pre-publication scrutiny of this book by a medical lawyer. In any case, quite apart from conflicts of legal opinion and interpretation, the law itself is constantly developing. Thus, if a formal legal opinion is required it will always be prudent to consult a medical law text or obtain an opinion from a medical defence organization or other medical lawyer.

Raanan Gillon
Emeritus Professor of Medical Ethics
Imperial College London
August 2004

About the authors

Lead author

Victoria Tippett is currently a pre-registration house officer in general medicine and infectious diseases at Ealing Hospital, London. She graduated in Healthcare Ethics and Law from the University of Manchester in 2000 and completed her medical studies at Imperial College, London in 2003. Alongside her enthusiasm for medical ethics and law are an interest in communication skills and in holistic patient care. She is a keen musician, radio presenter and debater.

Contributors

Thiraupathy Marianayagam is currently working as a pre-registration house officer in surgery at Wexham Park Hospital, having first worked in general and acute medicine at Ealing Hospital in London. She graduated from the University of Manchester in 2002 and Imperial College School of Medicine in 2003.

Louise Ma is currently in her medical pre-registration house officer post in renal medicine at Charing Cross Hospital NHS Trust. She graduated from Imperial College in 2003 and enjoyed a BSc at the University of Manchester in 2001. Her ambition is to have a career in medicine and she will be working at Lewisham Hospital in August 2004. She enjoys in-line skating and is a computer nerd at heart.

Acknowledgements

The completion of the text you hold in your hands would not have been possible without the support, enthusiasm and encouragement of many people. My interest in medical ethics and law was nurtured at the Centre for Social Ethics and Policy at the University of Manchester, and I would particularly like to thank Margot Brazier, John Harris, Charles Erin and Søren Holm for their encouragement. When ideas for the book were first discussed, Louise Ma and Thiraupathy Marianayagam were enthusiastic about the project from the start. Their sterling work was vital to the book, and I thank them for their ongoing support. As supervisor, mentor and kind teacher, Richard Ashcroft at Imperial College has backed my creation of this book from start to finish, and I thank him for his gentle words of wisdom.

The team at Radcliffe Publishing have been committed to this project and have supported me over several months. I would particularly like to thank Gillian Nineham and Paula Moran for their time and dedication.

Finally, my family, who have taken me through the darkest and most frustrating hours of writing and editing this book. In particular my mother, Marilyn, who has spent countless hours reading drafts, and my boyfriend, Alan, who has patiently discussed the book with me for months and persistently argued the utilitarian perspective at every opportunity. Thank you for your unstinting support, comfort and love.

The author of this book is not a lawyer and the contents serve merely as guidance in this area. If you require formal legal advice please consult your medical defence organization or a qualified lawyer.

CHAPTER 1

Truthfulness, trust and good communication

Victoria Tippett

Truthfulness is essential to the doctor–patient relationship, and to the trust which patients place in their doctors. If these vital elements break down the therapeutic relationship, which plays such a large role in how patients accept and respond to treatment, loses its strength. Clear and effective communication is at the heart of an honest doctor–patient relationship, but historically this has been ignored in medical education. The assumption has been made that all doctors have medical knowledge and are therefore intrinsically good communicators. New medical curricula are addressing this issue, although the manner in which communication skills are presented to students means that they are often taken less seriously than other more scientific studies. These efforts can only have a positive impact upon medical practice and the maintenance of honest, truthful relationships between patients and their doctors.

This chapter is more discursive and has less legal content than later sections, but covers important issues and relevant clinical situations. The topics explored include the ethical concept of paternalism, and how it is balanced with the rights of an autonomous patient, why truth matters, where truthfulness is difficult in everyday medical practice and why doctors lie, the boundaries of clinical discretion to withhold information, and how effective communication can build and maintain trust within the doctor–patient relationship.

Paternalism and autonomy

Paternalism: actions carried out for the protection of those seen to be vulnerable.

Autonomy: the right of an individual to exercise choice about any aspect of their life.

Doctors perceive their patients to be vulnerable and in need of their assistance and protection. This is unsurprising, as in most cases the doctor–patient relationship is initiated by the patient seeking advice and help from their doctor, and thus the stage is set for a paternalistic encounter. In recent times paternalism has been seen as a dirty word, and has been used when describing doctors as a group of arrogant and patronising individuals who interfere with and restrict their patients' choices. Whilst in some instances this is likely to be the case, it is an abuse of the term paternalism. It is not necessarily the case that the principles of autonomy and paternalism are in direct opposition.

It could be argued that paternalism lies close to the heart of medical practice, in that the actions of doctors are designed to protect and care for the sick – by definition a more vulnerable group in society. However, this does not necessarily mean that all sick patients have lost the ability to exercise their autonomy. By engaging with their patients and ascertaining their preferences and views, doctors can formulate plans of treatment that protect the vulnerable whilst respecting their wishes and allowing the patient to exercise their autonomy. In most everyday medical practice the wishes of the autonomous patient will not conflict with the advice of the paternalistic doctor.

As in much of ethics, there are limits to paternalism, just as there are limits to autonomy. Broadly speaking, autonomy ceases to be regarded once a patient is incompetent. From there on, decisions are made in that patient's 'best interests' – a paternalistic concept designed to protect the vulnerable incompetent patient. When a competent patient refuses a medical intervention, against the advice of their doctor, then autonomy is the overriding principle and the paternalistic wishes of the doctor are no longer important. These are, however, the black and white extremes of a broad grey area in which good communication can facilitate a balance between autonomy and paternalism.

Truth and trust

The doctor–patient relationship is built upon a foundation of trust, the essential component of which is the expectation that both parties will be truthful with each other. So fundamental is this concept that one of the duties of a doctor, as listed by the GMC, is to be 'honest and trustworthy'. In most cases this is not a problem – the patient feels it is in their best interests to tell their doctor the truth about their symptoms and the doctor feels it is in the patient's best interests to hear the truth about their condition. Cases in which the patient elects to lie to their doctor are beyond the scope of this chapter. However, there are many situations in which doctors feel it is in their patient's best interests for them to either lie or omit certain pieces of information.

Is an omission the same as a lie?

Debate is ongoing. Some argue that as omission is a failure to act, you are less culpable for an omission than for a lie, as that involves an act of dishonesty. Others argue that if the consequences are the same, the means by which they are achieved (either act or omission) is irrelevant. The limits of a doctor's discretion are outlined by the General Medical Council (GMC), British Medical Association (BMA) and ultimately the law, and are described later in the chapter.

What motivates doctors to lie to their patients?

When doctors give their patients information, it is usually only when that information is 'bad' news (as perceived by the doctor) that they will consider lying to their patient. It is this situation which is discussed below.

A combination of the principles of beneficence – acting to benefit your patient – and non-maleficence – to do your patient no harm – is often cited as a reason to lie. If you feel that terrible news would cause your patient significant psychological harm and may even adversely affect their prognosis, for example if they give up hope, you may lie to protect them from that harm. Although there is no research which supports the assertion that patients given bad news deteriorate more rapidly, this is a widely held belief amongst doctors.

Bad news for a patient can sometimes signify personal failure for their doctor, and requires that professional to accept that they are not in control of the situation and cannot solve everything. This may be a difficult position for the doctor – a person usually associated with successes and cures – to face, and so they may lie to their patient so that they do not have to deal with their own failure.

When breaking bad news to a patient, it is likely that the patient will have a significant emotional response to the information they receive. This may well be very difficult for the doctor to deal with. They are a person too (contrary to popular belief!) and the patient's distress can have a very negative impact upon their own emotional state. This is another factor that can make it easier for doctors to lie to their patients rather than to tell them the truth.

The legal limits of withholding information

The law recognises certain circumstances in which doctors may be justified in withholding information from their patients. These are clearly outlined and are supported by guidance from the BMA and GMC.

Patients require honest information about their diagnosis, prognosis, treatment options, likely treatment outcomes, common or serious side effects and timescale of treatment in order that they can give their informed consent to the treatment. UK law is not black and white when it comes to informed consent. To an extent, the *Bolam* principle applies. In its original form this states that:

'The test is the standard of the ordinary skilled man exercising and professing to have that special skill. A man need not possess the highest expert skill at the risk of being found negligent. It is a well-established law that it is sufficient if he exercises the ordinary skill of an ordinary man exercising that particular art.'[1]

In this case the above means that the information given to the patient must be that which most other doctors would give to their patients. However, in some cases, courts have ruled contrary to this, deeming that some risks ought to be disclosed to patients, even if most doctors would not make such disclosures.

'... the court must decide whether the information afforded to the patient was sufficient to alert the patient to the possibility of serious harm of the kind in fact suffered.'[2]

The GMC advises that patients have a right to information about healthcare services available to them, and that it should be presented in a way that is easy to follow and use. 'They also have a right to information about any condition or disease from which they are suffering. This should be presented in a manner easy to follow and use, and include information about diagnosis, prognosis, treatment options, outcomes of treatment, common and/or serious side effects of treatment, likely time-scale of treatments and costs where relevant. You should always give patients basic information about treatment you propose to provide, but **you should respect the wishes of any patient who asks you not to give them detailed information.**'[3]

The BMA has concerned itself with not just the situations discussed above, but also the economics of healthcare in the 21st century. Their guidance includes what patients should be told about the range of treatment options available to them when there is little or no likelihood that some of those options will be funded on the National Health Service (NHS). This encompasses not just embarrassing issues for doctors to discuss, but also areas of scientific uncertainty, and how this should be explained to patients in the context of novel unlicensed or experimental treatments.

The BMA currently advises that:

'Doctors should be as open as possible with their patients on clinical matters, whilst remaining aware of the particular needs of individual patients. Recognising the importance of informed and independent clinical judgement, the BMA considers there is no obligation for doctors to inform patients about treatments which the clinician believed would be futile for them.

Doctors should take their cue from patients as to the amount of information to impart about treatment options. Patients should have as much information as possible about why certain treatments were not available on the NHS (or through their insurer). In giving such information about the efficacy of the treatment for that individual, the strength of existing evidence about its effectiveness generally, and the financial constraints which control the availability of the treatment. [sic]

The public should be helped to gain awareness, in general terms, of issues of funding and rationing in the NHS. Concern has sometimes been expressed that clinical evidence about efficacy of some procedures is not being widely disseminated due to lack of funding.'[4]

Communication

It has long been recognised that the discrepancy in power and, often, in social class between the doctor and their patient has hindered effective communication. This is compounded, especially in urban areas, by an increasingly diverse population of patients. A patient's religious and cultural sensitivities will both affect the way in which they communicate with their doctor. On a practical level, many patients may speak little or no English, and interpretation facilities are stretched and limited. Communication is often, unsatisfactorily, conducted with a member of the family translating, and the patient's true narrative may be difficult to untangle from their relative's version of events. These are not excuses for poor communication between doctors and their patients, but an awareness of these issues can help doctors to overcome them. Communication skills are not something a person is born with – not even a future medical student – and development of these is a lifelong process.

Legally, if poor communication results in a patient not understanding a procedure, they cannot give their informed consent for it – even if they have signed the consent form. That consent would simply not be valid. In more everyday terms, effective communication is essential to the doctor–patient relationship and to maintaining the bond of trust that unites doctor and patient in a common cause.

Where you stand

- Doctors have a duty to be honest and trustworthy.
- Truthfulness is central to any encounter you have with a patient and to your therapeutic relationship with them.
- Patients must have honest and complete information in order that they can give their informed consent.
- Every patient should have basic information about the treatment you propose.
- If a patient asks you not to give them detailed information you should respect that wish.
- Every effort must be made to communicate effectively with your patient, being sensitive to cultural, gender, generational, religious and racial issues.

Where you fall

- If a patient does not understand or has not received all the necessary information about their treatment their consent will not be valid and you will be liable in negligence and/or battery.

Cases

> Mrs Smith is a patient of mine whom I have been treating with palliative therapy for an inoperable lung tumour. She is frail, and she knows that she has only a few weeks left to live. A recent set of investigations revealed that she has metastases in her liver. I have not told her about this – I feel it would only upset and distress her further – it would not be of any benefit to her. Do I have to give her the results?

In general, you should provide clear and honest information about Mrs Smith's condition to her. However, if you believe that her personal needs are best served by withholding her recent test results – and you would be prepared to justify your decision – then you may elect not to tell Mrs Smith about the liver metastases.

> Mr Singh is a patient of mine whom we recently diagnosed as having prostate cancer. When I spoke to him about his diagnosis, I explained that we

had found cancer. Before I had the opportunity to explain the diagnosis fully, outline his treatment options or explore his fears or concerns, he said, 'OK doctor, I know I have cancer, just get on and treat it. I don't want all the gory details. We'll just have to beat this'. I am worried that he does not fully understand what I told him, but he has refused any more information – what should I do?

If Mr Singh has been given basic information about his diagnosis and treatment, he is at liberty to refuse any further details and you should respect that wish. If you are unsure whether or not he understood the information you gave him, why not wait a short time and then ask Mr Singh what he understands about his problem, and whether he has any questions for you? This gives him the opportunity to either ask you for more details or to reconfirm his refusal of information. It is essential that you remember that refusal of treatment details is his right – however uneasy it may make you feel.

References

1   Bolam v Friern Management Committee (1957) 2 *All ER*: 118 at 121.

2   Sidaway v Board of Governors of Bethlem Royal Hospital (1984) *AC*: 871 at 903.

3   *Confidentiality: protecting and providing information*. Booklet produced by the General Medical Council.

4   http://www.bma.org.uk/ap.nsf/Content/Duty+of+candour?

CHAPTER 2

Consent

Victoria Tippett

Consent is often only thought of in the context of surgery or similar invasive procedures, but it applies to every activity which involves touching a patient. It thus includes many areas of routine medical practice, from conducting an abdominal examination or measuring a patient's temperature to administering an injection, taking blood or performing an appendectomy.

The term informed consent is often glibly bandied around, whilst being poorly understood by patients and doctors alike. In order for a patient's consent to be informed, they must be aware of the nature of the procedure and any significant risks which would 'affect the judgement of a reasonable patient'.[1]

The ethical background to the issue of informed consent lies in respect for a patient's autonomy, where autonomy is the right of an individual to make their own decisions about any aspect of their life. In this context it refers to the ability to have control over your own body and exercise self-determination. Thus a patient needs sufficient information, presented to them in an appropriate manner, to allow them to make decisions that will affect their bodily integrity.

The legal background covers areas of civil and criminal law. Although there is no statute which sets out the principles of consent, in common law (law that has developed based on previous cases) it has been established that touching a person (in this context, a patient) without a valid consent may constitute a battery under either the civil or criminal law. Also, if no valid consent is obtained and the patient suffers harm as a result of the treatment they have not consented to, they may bring a claim in negligence against the doctor performing the treatment. This is one of the reasons why it is increasingly emphasised within the NHS that the person who will perform the procedure should obtain the patient's consent, rather than leaving this task to a junior member of the team.

Although the guidance in this chapter accurately reflects the legal position at the time of writing, the area of consent is constantly evolving and it is important to consult the current Department of Health (DoH) or General Medical Council (GMC) guidelines regularly to remain aware of your legal position.

In particular, The Human Rights Act 1998 (which came into force in October 2000) is likely to affect medical law over the next few years, but even in 2004 it is too early to predict the impact that this Act will have.

What is a valid consent?

A consent is the permission a patient gives for a doctor to perform a specific action upon them. For that consent to be valid, it must be given **voluntarily** by someone who has both the **capacity to consent** to the proposed treatment and who has been **appropriately informed**. It is the three elements highlighted that are crucial to a valid consent, and they will be addressed individually.

Voluntary

The consent must be given voluntarily and freely. This means that the patient must not be under any pressure to accept or to refuse the treatment in question. It is not just doctors who can put such pressure on a patient, but also their friends, family members or partner, and doctors should be alert to these possibilities. Whilst guidance from others may be sought by the patient, the actual decision must be their own. If you think that pressure is being exerted upon a patient, you should make every effort to see them on their own, to establish that the decision is truly that of the patient themselves. In environments such as prisons or mental healthcare centres, there is the potential for patients to be coerced into consenting to treatments. Whilst it is important to separate coercion from giving appropriate advice to a patient regarding a particular treatment, coercion invalidates consent. A consent not freely and voluntarily given is not a valid consent.

Informed

Appropriate information is essential. It enables a patient to make informed decisions about their healthcare. A patient needs to understand in broad terms the nature and purpose of the procedure for which they are being asked to consent. This may include, where relevant, information about anaesthesia as well as information about the surgery itself. If any elements of this information are factually inaccurate or misrepresented, the consent will not be valid. In this area, the requirements of law in terms of battery differ from those regarding negligence. In terms of battery, to inform a patient of the nature and purpose of a procedure will enable a valid consent to be given.

This is, however, not enough to fulfil a doctor's legal duty of care. Therefore, if a doctor fails to provide any other relevant information they may be liable to a claim in negligence if the patient were to suffer any harm as a result of the treatment. So, for example, if you had explained to a man that his vasectomy was to prevent him ejaculating sperm and thus render him infertile, and that it would involve a local anaesthetic administered by injection to the groin, followed by two small incisions, one each side of the scrotum, to allow the tube carrying the sperm to be tied off on each side, you would have given him enough information in terms of a claim of battery. However, if you did not discuss with him the $1-2:1000$ risk of the operation failing and he subsequently fathered a further child, he would have a claim against you in negligence, as you failed to provide relevant information about risks of failure, and as a result he suffered harm.

There has been some difficulty in deciding what constitutes sufficient information to make an informed consent. Should the standard required reflect what the medical profession as a whole regard as acceptable practice or what patients feel is an acceptable amount of information? In other words, should it be the 'reasonable doctor' or the 'reasonable patient' who sets the level of sufficient information? Historically, the law erred on the side of the 'reasonable doctor'. They used the *Bolam Test*[2] which states: 'a doctor is not negligent if he acts in accordance with a practice accepted at the time as proper by a responsible body of medical opinion'. However, more recent cases have shown that whilst being influenced by standards set by the medical profession itself, the courts are prepared to challenge the views of a 'responsible body of medical opinion'. The courts will be the final arbiter of what constitutes responsible medical practice.

There is evidence that the shift towards a 'reasonable patient approach' continues. In a recent case it was stated that doctors should inform a patient of 'a significant risk which would affect the judgement of a reasonable patient'.[3] The GMC guidelines also advise that doctors should endeavour to ascertain a patient's individual needs and priorities when they provide them with information about the options for treatment (including no treatment at all). If a patient asks specific questions about the treatment and associated risks, the GMC advises that these should be answered truthfully.

Competent

A patient must be competent to consent to the particular treatment for their consent to be valid. This means that they must have the capacity to consent. In other words they must be able to understand and retain information which is material to the decision, and to weigh up this information when they make their choice. Generally, adults are presumed to have such capacity. Children lack the capacity to consent, and it is usually their parents who give consent on their behalf. However, this is an area of law all to itself, and will be discussed in Chapter 4 – Children, medicine and law. If a doctor is in doubt as to whether an adult has the capacity to consent, they should assess this and record the conclusions they draw in the patient's notes. It is important to facilitate consent as far as possible, for example by aiding patients with communication problems, and by taking care not to underestimate the capacity of patients with learning difficulties to understand. Advice from relatives and carers may help the doctor to maximise a patient's understanding and ability to give their consent.

If an adult patient is incapable of giving their consent because they lack capacity, the law states that nobody is able to give consent on their behalf. It is therefore not acceptable for the mother of a woman with severe learning difficulties who lacks capacity to consent to a sterilisation procedure on her daughter's behalf. At first sight, this may seem to deny many incapable patients treatment; however, in some circumstances such treatment is lawful without consent. The principle guiding treatment in these circumstances is the patient's *best interests*. These are not just their medical interests, but include the patient's values and preferences when competent (if the patient has subsequently lost capacity), their psychological health, well-being, quality of life, relationships, spiritual and religious welfare and their financial interests. In practice it is useful to involve patients' carers and relatives to discuss any preferences the patient may have had before they lost their capacity, unless the patient has previously made it clear that such individuals should not be involved in these decisions. In all cases it should be written in the patient's notes that they were unable to consent, and why the treatment was regarded as being in their best interests.

The doctors and relatives should not sign a consent form on the patient's behalf.

In certain circumstances, the courts have indicated that decisions about the care of incompetent patients *should* be referred to them. These are:

- sterilisation for contraceptive purposes
- donation of regenerative tissues such as bone marrow
- withdrawal of nutrition and hydration from a patient in a persistent vegetative state
- where there is doubt or confusion as to the patient's capacity or best interests.

If an adult is usually capable but temporarily loses their capacity to consent, for example whilst under sedation, in the absence of a valid advance refusal of treatment they may be treated. Such treatment must be necessary and no more than is reasonable in the patient's best interests pending that patient recovering capacity. If such treatment can reasonably be delayed until the patient regains capacity, it should not be undertaken until that time.

What if a patient refuses to consent?

If an adult with capacity makes a voluntary, appropriately informed decision to refuse treatment, even if this refusal may result in their death and/or the death of an unborn child (whatever the stage of pregnancy) then that refusal must be respected.

Equally, such a patient may withdraw their consent at any time, including during the performance of the procedure for which they originally consented. When a patient objects during treatment, if at all possible the doctor should stop the treatment and establish what the patient's concerns are, as well as explaining the consequences of not completing the procedure. If stopping the procedure would genuinely put the life of the patient at risk, the doctor may be entitled to continue until this risk no longer exists.

What if it's an emergency?

If it is an emergency and consent cannot be obtained, you may provide medical treatment to anyone who needs it. This treatment must be limited to that immediately necessary to save the life of the patient or avoid significant deterioration in their health.

Who should obtain a patient's consent?

It is the consultant in charge of a patient who is ultimately responsible for the quality of medical care provided, although it may be another member of their team who is performing the procedure. The GMC guidance advises that if you are the doctor providing the treatment, it is your responsibility to discuss it with the patient and obtain their consent. It suggests that this task should only be delegated where the person to whom the task is delegated:

- is suitably trained and qualified
- has sufficient knowledge of the proposed investigation or treatment, and understands the risks involved
- acts in accordance with the guidance in the GMC booklet 'Seeking patients' consent: the ethical considerations'.

It is important to remember that the seeking and giving of consent is not a one-off event but a continual process. It is good practice to seek consent for a procedure well in advance, and reconfirm this consent before the procedure starts.

Patients must not be given pre-operative medication before consent is sought for the procedure.

How important are consent forms?

The way a patient gives their consent is not important. Consent forms allow written consent to be taken routinely and in a standardised manner, but serve only as *evidence* of consent. If the criteria discussed above, of voluntary, informed consent by adults with the capacity to do so, have not been fulfilled, the signed consent form is simply invalid.

In certain circumstances, a consent form is a legal requirement but in general it is simply good practice to use them for treatments such as surgery. They are not generally a prerequisite and the lack of a consent form is no bar to treatment, provided that a valid consent has been given.

It is not just getting the patient to sign the form that gives you consent to perform the procedure. It is the patient having the capacity to consent, having been fully informed about the procedure and its attendant risks, having weighed the decision in their own mind and voluntarily chosen to consent to it which allows you to go ahead.

Additional points

Specific requirements surround medical research, live transplantation of human organs, gamete storage, subsequent use of removed tissue, self-harm, video recordings and clinical photography. Some of these issues are covered in Chapters 9 and 12, but any more information required can be found on the Department of Health website – http://www.doh.gov.uk.

 ## Where you stand

- Consent is necessary before you examine, treat or care for any competent adult patient.
- Adults are assumed to be competent unless you can demonstrate otherwise. If you have doubt ask whether they can understand and weigh up the information needed to make a particular decision about their care.
- Giving and obtaining consent is a continuous process, not a one-off event.
- Sufficient information must be given to a patient to allow them to weigh up the risks and benefits and any alternatives to treatment.

Where you fall

- To obtain consent is to respect your patient's autonomy – it is not just paperwork to allow you to get on with your treatment or protect you from a law suit.
- If your failure to obtain valid consent results in a lapse in the duty of care which you owe your patient, you will be liable in negligence and could face a legal claim.
- If your failure to obtain consent means that you commit a battery upon your patient, you will be liable under criminal law and could face a legal claim.
- Failure to obtain consent can result in disciplinary proceedings before the GMC and, ultimately, you could be struck off. This would leave you unable to practise medicine.

Cases

> I am the Senior House Officer (SHO) for a general surgical team. I often assist with procedures but never perform operations myself. Is it OK for me to get patients' consent for the consultant and registrar?

It is recommended that your registrar or consultant – whoever is actually performing the operation – obtains the patient's consent. With a busy surgical team this is not always possible. As long as you fulfil the criteria of being suitably trained and qualified, having sufficient knowledge of the proposed investigation or treatment, and understanding the risks involved, and you act in accordance with the guidance in the GMC booklet 'Seeking patients' consent: the ethical considerations', then you may obtain consent on their behalf.

> Mr Barker is due to have his inguinal hernia repaired. He has been nil by mouth since midnight and has just received his pre-operative sedatives. Yesterday afternoon I discussed the operation with him in detail, including what would happen, what the risks were and what his alternatives were. He was happy for the operation to go ahead, but I forgot to get him to sign the consent form. Should I get him to sign it now?

No! Firstly, the consent that Mr Barker gave you verbally yesterday is just as valid as a signed consent form – especially if you remembered to document this conversation you had with him in his medical notes. Secondly, he has now had his pre-operative sedatives and so is no longer competent to give a valid consent. Even if he signed the form, it would not be evidence of a valid consent.

Mrs Mazewicz attended her last outpatient appointment a month ago. At that visit I explained fully the process, alternatives, and risks of her forthcoming varicose vein operation to her. She was happy with the plan and freely consented to the operation. She came into hospital this evening, ready for tomorrow's operation, but is refusing to sign the Trust's standard consent form. Do I have to cancel her operation?

If the issue is simply that of signing the form, then no, the verbal consent that Mrs Mazewicz gave to you in the outpatients department is valid. However, if Mrs Mazewicz has changed her mind, and now withdraws her consent, then the operation must be cancelled. Consent is a continual process, and her agreement of a month ago is overridden by her refusal this evening. You must clarify whether her objection is to the operation itself or just the form. So long as she has the necessary capacity to consent, you must also respect her refusal or withdrawal of that consent.

References

1   Canterbury v Spence (1972) 464 F 2d 727 DC.

2   Bolam v Friern Management Committee (1957) *2 All ER*: 118 at 121.

3   Lord Woolfe MR in *Pearce v United Bristol Healthcare NHS Trust* (1999) *48 BMLR*: 118.

CHAPTER 3

Confidentiality

Victoria Tippett

Confidentiality is central to the trust a patient places in their doctor and thus to their therapeutic relationship. In all walks of life, information given or received in confidence for one purpose may not be used for a different purpose or passed to anyone else without the consent of the provider of the information. In medicine the doctor's duty of confidentiality to their patient is widely recognised and its scope and implications are frequently discussed. With all its exceptions and legal limitations, confidentiality can seem very confusing to the junior doctor. This chapter will steer you through all the law and guidance to leave you with three basic principles that let you know where you stand.

Most guidance on confidentiality comes from the Department of Health (DoH) and the General Medical Council (GMC) although there are also legal requirements. Beginning with the law on confidentiality in clinical practice, this chapter will go on to explore doctors' professional guidance in this area and will deal specifically with the Access to Health Records Act 1990, Access to Medical Reports Act 1988 and the Data Protection Acts of 1984 and 1998.

Basic law

Although breaches of confidentiality by doctors are usually dealt with by the GMC or National Health Service (NHS) Trust Internal Procedures, a **legal** claim may be brought if:

- the information divulged had the necessary quality of confidence
- the information was imparted in circumstances implying an obligation of confidence
- the breach of confidence has caused harm to the party who divulged the information.

It is the third criterion of those listed above – that the breach of confidentiality should have caused harm – which makes the law in this area difficult to use.

The courts have previously found that the doctor–patient relationship and information divulged therein fulfil these criteria. As long ago as 1974 a judge stated that:

> '... in common with other professional men ... the doctor is under a duty not to disclose, [voluntarily] without the consent of his patient, information which he, the doctor, has gained in his professional capacity, save ... in very exceptional circumstances.'[1]

The law may act either pre-emptively or retrospectively. It can prevent the unauthorised use of confidential information by issue of a court order or it can punish such use by the award of damages to the patient. In clinical situations the former is effectively useless. As for the latter, most breaches in confidentiality by doctors result in embarrassment or emotional upset to the patient, but the courts are reluctant to view this as harm for which the patient could be financially compensated. The result is that little case law in this area exists.

What case law there is suggests that if a doctor's breach of confidentiality resulted in harm to the patient concerned, they would have a claim in contract against the doctor. It is also thought by many[2] that the tort of negligence could be used to enforce a doctor's duty of confidence. In this way the protection of clinical information could be seen as part of the duty of care the doctor owes to her patient. However, the tort of negligence would also require the patient to prove damage as a result of the breach of confidence and, for the reasons described above, this is not usually possible.

Exceptions

Virtually all parties accept that the duty of confidentiality is not absolute. In general, exceptions to the duty of confidentiality have not been tested in a court of law, and so guidance on these matters comes from the GMC and DoH rather than from the courts. The overriding principle is that: **if a doctor believes that disclosure of confidential information is necessary, he/she must be able and prepared to justify his/her decision.**

The GMC has identified the following circumstances as exceptional and justifying disclosure of confidential information.

Other care providers

If a patient has consented to treatment it is not necessary to obtain express consent for relevant personal information to be shared with other team members involved in providing that care. However, the GMC advises that patients be made aware that this will occur, and that doctors explain why such information sharing is necessary. If a patient objects to any particular information being shared in this way, their wishes should be respected **unless to not inform others would put them at risk of death or serious harm**.

It should be noted that doctors must make team members who receive patients' personal information aware that it is given to them in confidence. This means that, for example, GPs must ensure that their receptionists are aware of their duty of confidentiality regarding the patient information that they handle.

Education/research/public health/audit

Where the disclosure of a patient's information is not connected to their treatment, in situations such as those listed above, the GMC advises that doctors:

1   seek patient consent to disclosure as far as possible, **even if it is deemed that the patient cannot be identified from the disclosure**
2   anonymise the data as far as is possible
3   keep disclosure to a minimum.

If a patient will be personally affected by the disclosure (for example, in the setting of occupational health) their express consent must be obtained. If the patient refuses to consent, disclosures may only be made if they are in the public interest. This is translated to mean that the disclosure must be needed to protect the patient or someone else from risk of death or serious harm. Ultimately only the courts can determine what the 'public interest' is. However, in practice if, following a breach of patient confidentiality, the GMC receives a complaint, it may require that the doctor concerned justifies her actions.

Those who cannot consent – children and adult patients may lack the competence to consent. This means that because of immaturity, illness or mental incapacity they cannot legally authorise the disclosure of their personal information.

Unconscious patients – a doctor may act without consent if she is proceeding with treatment necessary to preserve or prevent deterioration of the patient's physical or mental health.

Children – generally, children under 16 years of age may not consent. In such cases, their parents can consent to the disclosure of personal information on their child's behalf. If a child who is less than 16 years old is 'Gillick competent' (i.e. has achieved significant maturity and intelligence to enable them to understand fully what is proposed) then they may consent to the disclosure of such personal information.

Incompetent patients – the DoH states that:

'As the law stands, nobody is empowered to give consent on behalf of an adult. However, if a patient is unconscious or unable due to his or her mental or physical condition to give informed consent or to communicate a decision, decisions to pass on information will in practice usually be taken by the health professionals concerned, taking into account the patient's best interests and, as necessary, the views of relatives or carers. Such circumstances will usually arise when a patient has been unable to give informed consent to treatment. An earlier refusal to particular information being passed on, given while a patient had the capacity to decide, should, unless there are overriding considerations to the contrary, be regarded as decisive in circumstances similar to those envisaged by the patient.'[2]

Disclosure after death

The case law is also lacking in the area of disclosure of personal information after a patient's death, so again guidance comes from the GMC. They state that you retain an obligation to keep personal information confidential after a patient's death. The GMC also advise that you consider whether disclosure of information would cause distress to or be of benefit to relatives/the partner of the patient.

In certain situations you must divulge information about a deceased patient. You are legally obliged to provide relevant information to assist a coroner, procurator fiscal or similar officer in connection with an inquest or fatal accident inquiry. You are also legally obliged to enter relevant patient information on death certificates, which must be completed both honestly and fully. It is worth noting that in this way, disclosure can occur in a roundabout fashion, as death certificates are public documents and any person may approach the relevant official and ask to see one.

Compulsory disclosure

In addition to the circumstances just mentioned there are several instances, connected to judicial proceedings or statutory requirements, where a doctor **must disclose** patient information.

Statutory requirements

Infectious diseases

Notification of known or suspected communicable diseases is covered by the Public Health (Control of Disease) Act (1984) and specific forms are needed to report these cases. The form must be honestly completed and returned to the district Consultant in Communicable Disease Control. (The premise for this is that such carefully limited breaches of confidentiality are necessary to protect the health of the public at large, and are thus in the 'public interest'.)

Child protection

If you believe a patient to be a victim of neglect or physical, sexual or emotional abuse and that disclosure of personal information is in that patient's best interests, you should give this information promptly to the appropriate person or authority. Under the Children Act 1989 doctors have a duty to protect children who are their patients from abuse. In most cases you should tell your patient that you intend to disclose this information. Each area has a slightly different procedure in the area of child protection and doctors should contact their Area Child Protection Committee (ACPC) for local guidelines.

Abortion

Under the Abortion Act 1967 notice of a termination of pregnancy must be given to the relevant Chief Medical Officer.

Infertility

Under the Human Fertilisation and Embryology Act 1990 any children born as a result of infertility treatment must be registered with the Human Fertilisation and Embryology Authority (HFEA).

Births and deaths

Under the Birth and Death Registration Act 1953 all births and deaths must be notified to the local registrar. Every birth in England or Wales must be registered in the district in which it takes place within 42 days of the date of birth. Information for the registration is given to the registrar by the person registering the birth. Every death in England or Wales must be registered in the district in which it takes place within five days of the date of death. When someone dies, the doctor who was treating the deceased will issue a medical certificate of cause of death to the relatives. The person who will be registering the death must take this certificate to the registrar's office.

Drug addicts

Under the Misuse of Drugs Act (Notification of Supply to Addict) Regulation 1973, the treatment of drug addicts for their addiction must be reported to the Home Office.

Judicial requirements

You have a legal obligation to disclose information if ordered to do so by a judge or presiding officer of a court. You may object, if you feel that you are concerned, but ultimately the judge or presiding officer can compel you to disclose the information.

However, the above does not apply to disclosures to a third party, such as a solicitor, police officer or officer of the court. In these circumstances the patient's express consent is required, as previously described.

Access to medical reports

The Access to Medical Reports Act was passed in 1988. It applies to reports prepared by a doctor who has clinical charge of a patient, where the report will be directly supplied to the patient's employer or to an insurance company. Under the Act, the applicant must positively seek the patient's consent and must inform him of his rights to access. The patient may view the report before it is sent out. If necessary, the issue of the report may be delayed by up to three weeks to allow the patient to read the report. The patient may ask the doctor to alter anything they feel is inaccurate. If the doctor refuses to amend the report, the patient may add a statement to it, expressing their dissent.

If the doctor feels that disclosure of their report would cause serious harm to the patient's mental or physical health, or to that of any other person, they may refuse to allow the patient access to the report. In these circumstances, the patient may withdraw their original consent to the report and thus prevent it from being sent to the original applicant (e.g. their employer).

Access to health records

The Access to Health Records Act was passed in 1990 and applies to all notes made by a health professional in connection with the care of the patient after 1 November 1991. It allows patients not only to see records made about them by health professionals, but also to correct the information held if the patient feels it is inaccurate. If the healthcare professional who made the notes agrees to the patient's correction, the notes may be amended accordingly. However, if they do not agree, a note should be made in the relevant part of the notes, recording the patient's differing views. The only exemption from the above is records which the relevant healthcare professional feels would be likely to cause serious mental or physical harm to the patient if they were to have access to them. Records made before 1 November 1991 are not included under the Act, but if it is necessary to have access to these in order to understand records that fall under the Act, then access to these should be granted.

Although the law does not recognise a right to access records made before 1 November 1991, doctors and other healthcare professionals working in the NHS are required to release a patient's records to them, even if stored before 1995, if the patient asks for them. This is due to the 'Code of Practice on Openness in the NHS' which came into force in 1995. Although this code is not statutory and so has no legal power, it is enforceable by the Health Service Commissioner (see also Chapter 1).

Data protection acts

A patient's medical records also fall under the Data Protection Act 1998 that supplemented and reinforced the previous Act of 1984. It applies to both data stored on computer and information manually stored in filing systems. The Act gives the patient a right to information about why data about her are being stored, and who will have access to that information. Subject to an administrative fee, the patient has a right to be told by the 'registered data user' (the person or organization that holds their medical records) whether information about her is being held, and to be given a copy of the data. This is principally so that the patient can ensure the accuracy of the information on record.

 Where you stand

- Always get your patient's express consent to the disclosure of their personal information.
- If you believe the disclosure of confidential information is necessary, be able and prepared to justify your decision.
- Do not discuss your patient's personal information with their relatives unless you have your patient's express consent to do so.

 Where you fall

- The penalties for breaching confidentiality range from paying financial damages to a patient after a legal case to being struck off the medical register by the GMC.

Cases

My patient has recently been diagnosed with epilepsy. As he drives a car to work, I have informed him that he now has a legal duty to inform the Driver and Vehicle Licensing Agency (DVLA) about his condition. When I saw him yesterday and asked what the DVLA had said, he told me that he had not and would not tell them. He stated that he had driven for the last 20 years and as far as he was concerned he was a safer driver than most people on the roads. His epilepsy is difficult to control and he still experiences seizures. I do not feel he is safe to drive but he refuses to stop. What can I do?

The GMC guidelines are very clear in this situation:

'If patients continue to drive when they are not fit to do so, you should make every reasonable effort to persuade them to stop. This may include telling their next of kin. If you do not manage to persuade patients to stop driving, or you are given evidence that a patient is continuing to drive contrary to advice, you should disclose relevant medical information immediately, in confidence, to the medical adviser at the DVLA. Before giving information to the DVLA you should try to inform the patient of your decisions to do so. Once the DVLA has been informed, you should also write to the patient, to confirm that a disclosure has been made.'

My patient is suffering from hearing problems. I have offered to refer her for a hearing aid to be fitted but she refuses. I know that she works as a train driver and I am worried that her hearing is now so bad that she is putting her passengers at risk by continuing to work. I have tried to persuade her to talk to her employer about this but she refuses and tells me that they would simply sack her. What should I do?

Whilst you owe this patient the same duty of confidentiality as any other patient, she is, in your judgement, endangering the lives of others. If you cannot persuade her to tell her employer, you must inform her that you are going to tell them. You should explain to her your reasons for disclosing this information. Once you have contacted her employer, you should confirm to her in writing that a disclosure has been made.

I have just admitted an eight year old with severe pneumonia. On examination I noted that he had extensive bruising to his limbs and chest. When I asked him what had happened he remained silent. I later asked his mother, who told me that he fell downstairs. Although she seemed to be a concerned and caring parent, I am worried that the bruises might be the result of physical abuse. What should I do?

Each different area/trust has its own child protection policy and you should refer to that. In the first instance it will give you the name of a contact person in your area to discuss your worries with. They can then advise you as to what your next step should be. It is important to document all your examination findings in such a case (for example, drawing diagrams showing the extent of bruising) as you and other professionals may need to refer to these later if the case is taken further.

I was working late on the wards last night when I was stopped by a young man. He said he was the son of my patient, Mrs Shah, and could I please tell him what the results of her liver tests were. I didn't know what to say and, luckily, my bleep went off. When I returned from answering it, the man had gone. What should I have done?

Saved by the bell! In terms of both the law and the GMC guidelines it doesn't matter whether the young man really was Mrs Shah's son or not. You cannot disclose any personal information about Mrs Shah without her express consent. If she had asked you to explain her results to her family, you would have been at liberty to do so. However, if she had not you must not divulge any such information to her friends, relatives or any other enquirer. In such a situation you should encourage the young man to ask Mrs Shah herself about the test results. Whilst this may put you in a difficult situation occasionally, to divulge such results without your patient's permission is to breach confidentiality and so to break the law.

My patient, Mr Simpson, was being investigated after an episode of haemoptysis. Whilst we were not sure of his diagnosis we strongly suspected that he had lung cancer. The other evening, whilst I was covering the wards, his daughter asked for a quiet word with me. She expressed her concerns that her father has cancer. I explained that our team did not know the cause of his symptoms as yet. The daughter asked me not to tell her father any bad news. 'If it's cancer, let me deal with it – don't tell Dad. He's confused – he won't understand – and he'll only worry about it. He always worries. He'll probably worry himself to death. Please don't tell him,' she said. I explained that, as there are no results back yet there was no news to tell, good or bad, but Mr Simpson's daughter was insistent. I suggested '... that we wait and see what the investigations reveal?' and the daughter reluctantly agreed. We now have the results of our investigations which confirm that Mr Simpson has lung cancer. My consultant has asked me to pass this news on to his daughter if I see her whilst on call tonight as the

next ward round is not until the day after tomorrow. I do not think that
Mr Simpson is too confused to understand his diagnosis but both my consultant and his daughter do not want me to tell him. What should I do?

If Mr Simpson is deemed incompetent, decisions can then be taken on his behalf
in his 'best interests'. However, until such an assessment has taken place he is
owed the same duty of confidentiality as any other patient. Therefore only Mr
Simpson can consent to you telling his daughter about the results.

Given the above position in law, you may choose to tell Mr Simpson nothing (but not lie to him if he asks directly) until your consultant explains the
results to him on her ward round. Whatever you choose, you must not discuss
the results with his daughter. Without Mr Simpson's express consent such a
discussion would breach the duty of confidentiality which you owe to him as
your patient.

References

1   Hunter v Mann (1974) 1 *QB*: 767 at 772.

2   'The Protection and Use of Patient Information: Guidance from the Department of Health'
Section 4.9 at http://www.doh.gov.uk

CHAPTER 4

Children, medicine and law

Victoria Tippett and Thiraupathy Marianayagam

Changing attitudes in recent decades have led to increased interest in the ethical and legal position of children in society. Whilst few would be at ease with the thought of children being accorded the full spectrum of rights that adults currently enjoy, there is a growing body of opinion that their interests should be considered and respected independently from those of their parents or guardians.

Children are a vulnerable group. They are, in general, not thought to be competent to make significant decisions about their well-being since they lack the ability to analyse the possible consequences that may arise. Since they are not able to make these decisions, they do not have to take responsiblity for the choices that are made on their behalf. However, with age and experience they gradually begin to acquire the skills required and start to become more autonomous. Many situations do occur within the medical field when this assertion of self-determination by the child runs counter to the wishes of their parents or guardians.

Parental responsibility

Children (at least the very young of this category) are generally unable to give valid consent for their treatment. This duty is therefore passed on to their parents or other adults who possess parental responsibility for them. This responsibility encompasses decisions that are made in all aspects of a child's life such as medical treatment and education. Parental responsibility allows parents to bring up their children in the way that they see fit. It is an automatic right and is not easily overridden. Whilst it may be difficult to agree with the way in which certain parents choose to bring up their children, their choice cannot be denied unless it can be shown that the child's welfare is harmed.

With regard to medical intervention, any adult with parental responsibility is allowed to give proxy consent on behalf of a child. The rules regarding who has this power are outlined in the Children Act 1989.

1   The parents of a child who are married either before or after the birth of that child. This responsibility is not altered by divorce, separation or in the event of the child being taken into care. It is only completely lost when a child is adopted.

2   The birth mother of the child assumes automatic parental responsibility. The unmarried father can only assume responsibility by:

- marrying the child's mother
- formally adopting his child
- being appointed its legal guardian
- signing and officially recording a parental responsibility agreement or a residence order with the child's mother.

3   Other parties (step-parents, relatives, etc.) can assume responsibility by:

- residence orders
- adoption
- appointment as guardians
- emergency protection orders.

In this scenario, parental responsibility is granted to the other parties alongside the existing parents.

There are often situations in which immediate decisions must be made by someone with parental responsibility. A child who falls ill at school, for example, may need medical attention. Someone may be required to consent to their treatment *in loco parentis*.

The adult in charge of the child at that time does not have immediate parental responsibility, but they do have the right to act in the child's best interests at that time. This principle of necessity is similar to that applied to justify the treatment of an unconscious patient.

Consent to treatment

All medical treatment requires informed consent from the patient. However, children cannot give a valid informed consent and so proxy consent is required from their parents.

Whilst it is in the parents' power to refuse treatment on behalf of their children, it is important to realise that their primary duty, in the eyes of the law, is to consider the best interests of their child.

The obvious problem with this consideration of 'best interests' is its extremely subjective nature. The parents' personal beliefs and experiences may lead them to choose a different path from that of the medical staff. In 2001, such a difference of opinion led to St Mary's Hospital, Manchester seeking the court's permission to separate Siamese twins, Mary and Jodie, after their parents refused to give their consent. The court ruled that doctors could operate on the twins despite their parents' refusal to consent to the operation. Religious and cultural attitudes commonly lead to the refusal of certain types of treatment. Jehovah's Witnesses are known to refuse blood products and will also refuse such products for their children.

The action that the doctors want to pursue may in itself be simple and not immediately life-saving, such as a blood test. The results of it could, however, be of the greatest importance. Parents who refuse to allow their child to be tested for human immunodeficiency virus (HIV) infection are seen to be blocking that child's potential treatment. They could argue that the medication would be toxic to their child, with severe side effects. The knowledge that their child was HIV positive would be stigmatising and the degree of intrusion into their lives would be a constant reminder of their child's illness. Their view of their child's best interests encompasses more than just the medical condition. They know their child and their social situation better than the doctors do and so feel that they are the best judges of the situation.

The doctors may disagree. They may feel that there is a good chance that this child will survive with a good quality of life if she is treated with the necessary medication. They will be able to monitor her condition and hopefully resolve any future complications quickly before they become very serious. This is a situation that has arisen before and it is likely that similar cases will appear in the future as parents are gaining more confidence and refusing treatment against the advice of their doctors.

Whilst doctors will accommodate parental wishes as far as possible, they must not compromise the child's health. They must ultimately act in the child's best interests, even if this involves ignoring parents' wishes. Doctors can apply to the High Court to exercise its inherent jurisdiction to override the child's parents.

There are also situations in which one parent may be willing to give their consent even if the other adamantly refuses it. Section 2(7) of the Children Act 1989 gives every parent the right to independent action. Therefore, technically doctors can act on the consent of one parent even if they know that the other is against the action. However, it is easy to see that many medical professionals may feel uneasy about treating a child in the face of such resistance.

Can children ever consent for themselves?

All those under the age of 18 are minors in the eyes of the law. However, for the purposes of medical treatment, those over the age of 16 can give consent which cannot be overridden by their parents (Counter-intuitively they cannot refuse treatment. For more details see pages 30–1). Children under the age of 16 are not capable of giving valid consent, unless they can be shown to have the maturity to be able to reach those decisions themselves. The age at which this occurs varies from child to child and is also dependent to a degree on the decision that needs to be made. A younger child may be able to consent to minor treatment such as a blood test but may not be able to understand the need for transplant surgery. This ability to give an informed and thus valid consent is known as 'Gillick competence'.

In 1985, Mrs Gillick brought forward a case against her local health authority. The Department of Health and Social Security (DHSS) had issued guidelines to doctors regarding teenage sex education and treatment. They decided that it would be acceptable for doctors to provide minors with advice and treatment for contraception without the consent or knowledge of the parents if this was what the minor wanted. Mrs Gillick felt that this was against parents' right to consent to any treatment for their children. The decisions made in that case have had a major bearing on children's rights ever since. By a majority of 3:2 in the House of Lords, Mrs Gillick's case was lost. The decisions that were given stated that parental rights did not disappear overnight, rather that they slowly diminished with the increasing maturity and responsibility of the child in question. Whilst parental consent should always be sought, the sufficiently mature older minor can consent for themselves. They are also in a position to request a degree of confidentiality from their parents or others.

Whilst 'Gillick competence' was devised with regards to contraceptive issues, it has been widely used in paediatric cases. There are no hard and fast rules as to how to judge 'Gillick competence', although it has been posited that it is highly unlikely that any child under the age of 12 has sufficient maturity to be considered capable of giving valid consent. The child should have reached a degree of understanding and intelligence which allows him to make a decision for himself after considering all the facts put forward to him. There is no clear guidance dictating how much allowance should be made for other factors such as the influence of his parents and family, stress or illness, social circumstances or even mental or physical health. The older child may disagree with his parents or side with them against his doctors. In either case, he has a view about his best interests that must be taken into account by all concerned. If it is agreed that the child is 'Gillick competent', then his consent, or refusal of it, is legally valid and may not simply be overturned by his parents.

Whilst Gillick provides that a child can consent to treatment, it is less clear as to what should happen if consent is denied. If a child does refuse consent, can this consent be obtained from another source? The courts have the power of *parens patriae* which enables them to make decisions on behalf of those under the age of 18 who require protection. This is not a blanket power to allow all doctors to have their preference accepted over those of others, nor is it a guarantee that parents can use it to force their children to have the treatment option that they themselves feel is the best course of action. It is true that the majority of cases have found that in cases of conflict, particularly where there is dissent between the child and the doctors, the courts have found in favour of the medical profession but this could easily change. Cases are still taken to court by children who adamantly believe that they are correct in their evaluation of their best interests. It could be that doctors are more willing to listen to children and their parents and so come up with alternative treatment options. This less paternalistic practice of medicine may lead to only those cases in which no other path is viewed as possible by the healthcare professional being taken as far as the courts. If this is true, then the attitudes of those in the medical profession have changed significantly to acknowledge patient autonomy. The courts must act in accordance with the best interests of the child and will take into account all points of view before reaching a decision.

At present, the law does not accept that the ability to consent to treatment automatically gives a minor the right to refuse the treatment.

So how do I judge which children are 'Gillick competent'?

The children in question will be between 12 and 16 years old. Those younger are always considered too young to make such decisions while those over 16 already have the legal power to consent for themselves.

Ask yourself:

Does the child have sufficient understanding and intelligence to understand fully the medical treatment proposed?

If the answer is yes, you must consider the treatment proposed. The decision is ultimately a clinical one and it is only in exceptional circumstances that you will need to proceed with the child's consent alone. If the child fulfils the above criteria, and you cannot persuade them to involve their parents, you may legally proceed with the child's consent alone.

Investigating child abuse

All suspicions and allegations of child abuse must be treated seriously and promptly. The healthcare team are, under these circumstances, able to share information with other relevant parties without any parental consent, on the grounds of necessity.

Child protection is covered in Section IV of the Children Act. There are a number of measures available in order to guide the investigations of child abuse and neglect.

Child Assessment Order (CAO)

- This order allows for a child to be reviewed in terms of her health, development or treatment. Its purpose is to allow for decisions to be made regarding future action.
- The order is strictly court controlled and is used when there is serious concern over the child's well-being such as reports from school or neighbours. There must be some evidence that concern is warranted over the well-being of the child before an assessment order is granted.
- The assessment is 'child specific' and does not allow the whole family to be investigated, including other children.
- The order lasts for seven days but need not begin immediately. Since this is such a short period of time, it may be necessary to delay it until all the necessary professionals are able to be present.

Emergency Protection Order (EPO)

This order is used when serious concerns over a child's welfare warrant immediate action. It can be granted on three grounds:

1 serious harm is feared if the child is not immediately removed
2 frustrated access where the local authorities are denied access to the child when necessary
3 frustrated access where authorised personnel (other than the local authority) are unreasonably hindered when trying to make enquiries.

The access denied can only be considered frustrated if there were no reasonable explanations for it. An EPO can be used to prevent a child being removed from hospital by her parents if there is reason to believe that doing so would cause harm to the child.

Child abuse concerns can be voiced by anyone. However, once an investigation is under way they will be headed by specially trained professionals in collaboration with other authorities such as the police or local authorities.

Whilst it is extremely important that suspected child abuse cases are investigated, it should also be remembered that accidental injuries do happen. Accusations regarding child abuse may lead to innocent parents feeling unable to seek medical care in the future for fear of stigmatisation. However, as recent cases have shown, missing a diagnosis of neglect or abuse can lead to terrible consequences with the child as the victim.

What do I do if I suspect that a child is being abused?

Always refer to your local Area Child Protection Committee (ACPC) procedures.

General advice:

1   discuss difficult/worrying cases with your local senior paediatrician/designated doctor in child protection, senior colleagues or social services
2   if you are told of abuse or you strongly suspect it you will have to make a child protection referral to social services. It is *good practice* to inform the parents/carers/child that you are making this referral
3   make an enquiry of the local child protection register. (This allows information and concerns about a particular child or family to be shared.)

Do not be deterred by a lack of information – still make a referral to social services if you think a child has been or is being abused.

Always confirm verbal discussions and referrals in writing. Note everything carefully, with dates, times and names included.

Physical abuse

If the child needs hospital treatment/investigations then information should be shared with the hospital staff looking after the child. If you were the person who had initial contact with the child, you should contact the social services team as soon as possible.

   If no treatment is needed but abuse is strongly suspected, contact social services. If you are unsure, get a second medical opinion.

Sexual abuse

Any clear statement made to you of sexual abuse **must** be referred to social services/the police (as per your local procedure). Allegations of sexual abuse should also be referred – healthcare professionals do not have any statutory duties of investigation.

Do not ask detailed questions of the child as they will be interviewed later by investigating professionals. Ask what is necessary to determine the nature of the abuse and assess whether the child needs urgent medical treatment. Limit your physical examination to assessing and managing any acute injuries. A police surgeon or forensic examiner and paediatrician will jointly examine the child later in relation to the abuse.

Neglect/emotional abuse

Discuss any concerns you have with other team members, the designated child protection doctor and social services. Note carefully the chronology of events/incidents.

Any healthcare professional who is asked to examine a child in these situations, indeed when asked to examine any child, should always establish who has parental responsibility and the right to consent to treatment before proceeding.

 Where you stand

- Those under 16 years of age usually need their parents' or guardian's consent for medical treatment.
- If parents refuse to consent to vital treatment for their child you should apply to the High Court for an order to allow you to override their refusal.
- If a child is between 12 and 16 years old and 'Gillick competent' they may consent to treatment for themselves.
- If you suspect a child is being abused you must take action. Follow your local area Child Protection Guidelines.
- Remember – the welfare of the child always comes first.

 Where you fall

- If you do not obtain consent to treatment from a child's parent or legal guardian you will be liable in negligence and/or battery.
- If you obtain consent from someone with no legal power to give that consent (such as an unmarried father with no legal parental responsibility) you will be liable in negligence and/or battery.

- If you act contrary to a child's best interests, either with or against their parents' wishes, you will be failing in your duty of care for the child and will be liable in negligence.
- If you fail to act on suspicions or allegations of child abuse, you will be failing in your duty of care for the child and will be liable in negligence.

Cases

Oliver, a ten-year-old school boy, was brought in to see me in casualty by his teacher. He has had a nasty fall and appears to have broken his arm. The school and the hospital are unable to contact his parents. Oliver needs medical treatment, but who can I get to consent to it?

Section 3(5) of the Children Act allows Oliver's temporary carer, his teacher, to consent on behalf of his parents to 'do what is reasonable in all the circumstances of the case for the purpose of safeguarding or promoting the child's welfare'. The treatment that can be carried out should be that which is considered necessary. Anything that is not urgent and can wait until his parents give consent should be delayed.

Oliver's parents are not married. His father is already at the casualty department but his mother isn't here yet. Is he able to consent on behalf of his son?

With unmarried parents, only the mother automatically has the right of parental consent. Oliver's father can consent to treatment if he has a parental responsibility agreement with his mother.

My patient is Julia, a 13-year-old girl, who is in hospital for routine surgery. Her mother, a Jehovah's Witness, has consented to the operation being performed but refuses to consent to the use of blood products. The surgeon (my consultant) is unwilling to proceed with the operation without permission to do a blood transfusion if needed. How should I proceed?

The possible need for a blood transfusion and the reasons for it should be carefully and objectively explained to Julia and her parents. The necessity of the operation should also play a significant role in any decision made. Julia's father can give his consent to the operation, even if her mother is unwilling. Julia herself may be judged to be 'Gillick competent' and so consent to the use of blood transfusions herself. If no consent is forthcoming from any of these three individuals, then you may feel that the operation is serious enough to warrant legal proceedings to try and obtain consent through the courts.

✳ Alice is 15 and has discovered that she is pregnant. She wants an abortion but her parents refuse to consent to it on religious grounds. Alice has told me, as her GP, that she does not feel that she can look after a child and still finish school. She is scared of what is happening to her and the confrontations with her parents over the issue are very stressful to her. Can I refer her for an abortion?

Once again, Alice can consent to an abortion if she is 'Gillick competent' and fulfils the criteria in the Abortion Act 1967. Her parents will not be able to override this consent unless a court agreed with them that her decision was not in her best interests. If Alice is not thought to be 'Gillick competent', then she would have to use legal proceedings to obtain the court's consent to abort her pregnancy. Once again she would be required to demonstrate to you that it was in her best interests and complied with the Abortion Act 1967.

Sarah, a four-year-old girl, was brought in to see me (her GP) with a throat infection. Whilst examining her, I noticed that she has some painful bruising on her arms and legs. Her mother, Ellie, explained to me that her daughter is always running into furniture and hurting herself, but I am not convinced by this explanation. What should I do?

You should try to obtain Ellie's consent to examine Sarah more fully. This is a difficult situation and requires a lot of tact and understanding. Throwing accusations will be detrimental to the doctor–patient relationship with Ellie and is ultimately hurting Sarah the most. If you feel that your concerns have some justification, then you should contact an agency with powers to intervene and investigate. You cannot legally insist that Sarah be taken to hospital. If Ellie refuses to consent to Sarah being investigated then a CAO may be necessary with an EPO if it was then deemed that she was in imminent danger or if her parents continued to deny access for an examination.

CHAPTER 5

Mental health

Victoria Tippett and Thiraupathy Marianayagam

It is clear that there is a common theme running through the application of the law and ethics to medicine, namely that of informed consent to any treatment that takes place. Psychiatry, however, is one field in which much of the treatment is involuntary.

In paediatrics, the *parens patriae* (parent of the country) principle allows the court to consent to or refuse treatment on behalf of a minor or to appoint a legal guardian to do this. Whilst this used to apply to the treatment of incapable adults too, the Mental Health Act (MHA) 1959 first swept this provision away. There is therefore no legal jurisdiction in English law that allows consent to be given on behalf of the incompetent adult. This can lead to some legally grey areas concerning the treatment of those who cannot, or will not, give their consent.

The MHA 1983 sets out the guidelines concerning the treatment of the mentally ill in England and Wales. At its heart is the principle that all patients should be given the information they need to help them understand the nature of their illness, the treatment they need and how it will affect them. It reminds us that the mentally ill are vulnerable, require respect and should be helped to make as many autonomous decisions as they can.

The MHA defines four categories of mental disorder:

1 mental illness
2 mental impairment
3 severe mental impairment
4 psychopathic disorder.

Whilst there is no specific definition of mental illness in the MHA, it should be noted that deviant behaviour (sexual deviance, drug and alcohol abuse, etc.) do not constitute a mental disorder on their own.

Treatment

Patients fall into two categories for the purposes of treatment depending on how they came to be in hospital:

1   voluntary or informal admission
2   compulsory admission.

Informal admission

Patients who understand that they have some form of mental disorder and are willing to comply with a treatment regime are considered to be informal patients. At times, it may be felt that they would be better treated if they were admitted into hospital. If they agree to this course of action, or ask for it themselves, they are considered to be an informal admission. This is covered by Section 131 of the MHA 1983.

The compliant incapacitated patient, i.e. those who do not object to hospital admission but are incapable of giving consent, have fallen into a grey area. Does the fact that they do not object to hospital admission mean that they should be treated as informal admissions or does this mean that they are incapable of realising the need for treatment and therefore should be treated as compulsory admissions?

The case of *R v Bournewood Community and Mental Health Trust ex parte L* (1998) 2 *FLR*: 550 highlighted this particular problem. The Court of Appeal pointed out the dangers in categorising these patients as informal admissions in that they would not be protected in the same way as other vulnerable patients who were sectioned under the compulsory admission status. The House of Lords ultimately decided that those who are incapable of giving a valid consent could be treated as informal patients so long as they were complying with treatment.

Detention under the MHA 1983

Compulsory admission procedures (sectioning) are used when there is sufficient concern about a patient's condition to warrant their admission into hospital for their own safety, health and well-being and that of those around them for the purposes of assessment or treatment. Medical treatment is defined as including nursing, habilitation, rehabilitation, physical treatment such as medication or electro-convulsive therapy (ECT).

Tables 5.1 and 5.2 identify the various key sections available within the MHA 1983.

Table 5.1

MHA section	Purpose of the section	Section authorised by	Duration	Appeal
2	Assessment (plus urgent treatment)	2 approved doctors following application by an ASW or NR	28 days	Patient can appeal to MHRT within first 14 days
3	Treatment	Consultation by ASW or NR	6 months	Can appeal to MHRT at any time
4	Emergency assessment	1 doctor – preferably with previous knowledge of patient	72 hours. Premise is that assessment more urgent than sec 2	

Key:
MHRT – Mental Health Review Tribunal
NR – Nearest relative
ASW – Approved social worker (i.e. a social worker who is trained to assess whether a patient may need sectioning)

Table 5.2

MHA section	Purpose of the section	Section authorised by	Duration
136	Removal to a place of safety (for assessment) from a public place	Police officer	72 hours
135	Removal to a place of safety from private property	Police officer with magistrate's warrant	72 hours
5(2)	Any hospital inpatient needing urgent detention	Doctor currently caring for that patient	72 hours to be assessed for S 2 or S 3
5(4)	Inpatient being treated for a mental disorder – urgent detention needed in the absence of a doctor	Registered mental nurse	6 hours

Suffering from a mental illness does not automatically lead to incompetence to provide a valid consent. Internment under the MHA applies only to the treatment of the mental disorder and not to any other medical conditions that the patient may also have at that time.

The case of C, an adult patient suffering from chronic paranoid schizophrenia, is a good example of this. C was detained at Broadmoor Prison where he was compliant with his psychiatric medication and was making good progress. During his time at Broadmoor he developed a gangrenous foot. He was removed to a general hospital and the consultant caring for C gave him just a 15% chance of survival if he did not have a below-knee amputation of the gangrenous limb. C refused to have the operation and claimed that he would rather die with two feet than live with one, but his doctors questioned C's capacity to consent. An application for an injunction to restrain the hospital from carrying out the operation was made on behalf of C and was lodged with the court.

The courts ruled in C's favour. The reasons are clearly expressed by Thorpe J:

'... I am completely satisfied that the presumption that C has the right to self-determination has not been displaced. Although his general capacity is impaired by schizophrenia, it has not been established that he does not sufficiently understand the nature, purpose and effects of the treatment he refuses. Indeed, I am satisfied that he has understood and retained the treatment information, that in his own way he believes it, and that in the same fashion he has arrived at a clear choice.'

Re C (adult refusal of medical treatment) (1994) 1 *All ER:* 819 at 824.

The three-stage test that was applied to the case was:

1 can the adult patient comprehend and retain the treatment information given to him?

   C was an intelligent individual and the courts felt that he had completely understood the reasons for his treatment and illness.

2 does the patient believe the information given to him?

   C did believe that the treatment offered to him was valid, but argued that it was not the only option open to him.

3 can the patient weigh it in the balance to arrive at a fully informed choice?

   The court decided that C was capable of doing this, despite his mental health disorder.

There are times when the treatment of physical symptoms is closely related to the treatment of the mental condition. Some mental disorders such as anorexia nervosa illustrate this well. Here, the force-feeding of the patient has been justified on two counts. Firstly, it is necessary treatment to save the life of that individual and secondly, it is a treatment for that particular psychiatric illness. However, is feeding a treatment of the mental symptoms or is it primarily aimed at reducing the physical symptoms such as weight loss and its associated problems?

Many legal cases have been brought involving compulsory feeding of minors (those aged less than 16). Minors who refuse to enter hospital for the treatment of their anorexia nervosa may try to avoid compulsory detention through the courts. However, they have, as yet, rarely succeeded. In one such case, the Court of Appeal decided that a feature of anorexia nervosa was that it affected the ability to make an informed choice; thus refusing to accept this specialist treatment was thought to be akin to refusing treatment for a mental disorder. In cases involving adults, since the courts have no power to force treatment, they must decide that the non-consensual treatment used in this illness falls under the remit of the MHA. In another case involving a 37-year-old woman, the judge ruled that:

> 'I have no difficulty at all in concluding ... that feeding is treatment within s 145 of the 1983 Act. It is an essential part of nursing and care. It is more difficult to decide whether it constitutes medical treatment for the mental disorder. The disorder is anorexia nervosa ... [The medical evidence] is clearly not the effect that feeding a person suffering from anorexia nervosa is an essential part of that treatment.'[1]

Treating the mentally disabled

The issue of treating the mentally incompetent can become very complex. Whilst the doctors should always consult the patients and their families as far as possible, it is important to note that proxy consent cannot be given for anyone over the age of 18, even if they are permanently unable to give it themselves. For example, the mother of a child born with cerebral palsy and learning disability cannot consent on her daughter's behalf. In law, a doctor can provide treatment for a mentally handicapped person without consent, so long as to receive that treatment is in the patient's best interests.[2] Obviously, the mentally incompetent patient may well suffer from a physical condition unrelated to their mental disorder which should be treated, but what about conditions which are not so detrimental to the patient's immediate health?

The sterilisation of mentally incompetent patients is one such example. In the past widespread sterilisation of the mentally incompetent took place. In the United States this was criticised as a form of eugenics. The issue illustrates the tension between the rights to maintain bodily integrity, to procreate and to be able to mix freely within the community without the need to suffer the consequences of pregnancy (which may not be understood by the individual).

The families and doctors who request permission to carry out sterilisation are often considering the fact that the patient would, in their opinion, be unable to cope with being pregnant. Occasionally, they are also aware that if the individual knew that she was pregnant then she would be likely to refuse to have an abortion. In law, they should have considered other forms of contraception but these may have been ruled out because of existing medical conditions (for example, those with epilepsy might not be able to take contraceptive medication). Relying on the mentally disabled individual to use barrier methods of contraception is also not deemed to be practical – many adults who are considered to be competent have found such methods to be unreliable themselves. It may be hard to allow mentally incompetent individuals to enjoy their lives without the knowledge that they will not be burdened with an unplanned pregnancy which they could not cope with.

These reasons are all very powerful ones but it should be remembered that sterilisation is a permanent barrier to reproduction, one of the most basic rights protected by the Human Rights Act. It should only be considered as a last resort, even if there are some practical difficulties with other forms of contraception. Whilst it may prevent an unplanned pregnancy, it will not prevent sexual abuse from taking place nor the risk of sexually transmitted disease. It has also been suggested that sterilisation would in fact mean that anyone taking advantage of the mentally disabled woman could do so in the knowledge that she would not be made pregnant.

The cases of sterilisation for the mentally handicapped have brought to the fore the inadequacies of the law regarding consent to treatment for this group of people. Whilst changes have been implemented, designed to improve the autonomy of the mentally handicapped or mentally ill, there are still areas where a paternalistic approach seems to be the only option currently available. Again, the emphasis within this approach must be on the best interests of the patient. Currently, the decision is left to the patient's doctors, who are expected to act on their patient's behalf according to their needs. Families will expect to have a significant input into the decision-making process, since any action taken could have serious implications for them as well, **but the patient's needs must be considered above all others**.

Principles to consider when making decisions on behalf of the mentally incompetent:

- what is the aim of the treatment?
- is it necessary for the health and well-being of the patient?
- whose benefit is the treatment aimed at? (Sterilisation, organ donation and research studies can all be seen as having more benefit to others

than to the mentally handicapped patient who may be unaware of the benefit they receive.)

- what are the patient's past and present wishes?
- are these wishes reasonable in the light of the situation currently faced?
- has the situation been explained as fully as possible to the patient?
- have their feelings and opinions been taken into account?
- have the feelings and opinions of other appropriate people been taken into account such as their family, carers and other closely involved health-care staff?
- what are the practical considerations of the treatment proposed?
- are there any other treatment options which would be as effective?
- how will any disputes which arise between those who are consulted be resolved?
- are there any social, religious or cultural factors which could have a significant effect on the patient's best interests?

 # Where you stand

- A patient may be sectioned under the MHA 1983 if there is sufficient concern about their condition to warrant their admission into hospital for their own safety, health and well-being and that of those around them, for the purposes of assessment or treatment.
- The MHA does not cover compulsory treatment of conditions other than their mental health problems.
- A patient willing to comply with treatment but incompetent to consent to their admission may be treated as an informal patient, for so long as they continue to comply with treatment.
- Nobody can give proxy consent for a mentally incompetent adult.
- A doctor may treat a mentally incompetent adult so long as the treatment is in that patient's best interests.
- Cases involving sterilisation of a mentally incompetent person should always be taken to the courts.

 # Where you fall

- Mental health is tightly governed by the law and it is vital that you keep well informed and up to date with current legislation.

- Wrongful detention is a serious offence.
- To obtain consent from a patient who is incompetent to give it will result in your being liable in negligence and/or battery.
- To treat a competent patient detained under the MHA for treatment unrelated to their mental health problems and against their consent will result in your being liable in negligence and/or battery.

Cases

Tom is a 26-year-old man with Down's syndrome. He lives in sheltered accommodation and has a part-time job in a shop. His sister Claire is 34 years old and lives nearby. She has been his main carer for many years and sees him every day when he comes to her house for dinner with her family. Whilst Tom has a high degree of freedom, he is very dependent on Claire. Claire has renal failure and is in need of a kidney transplant. She has been on the waiting list for some time, but no suitable kidneys have been found yet. Tom is her best match. Her children are willing to donate but they are both under the age of 16. Of her other blood relatives, there is no other suitable match amongst those who were willing to be tested. Tom does not understand the situation enough to be able to give consent to donate his organ.

Can Claire receive a donation from him despite his lack of informed consent?

There is no 'right answer' in a scenario like this. No such case has ever come to court and it is difficult to second-guess what the result would be. On balance, whatever the ethical arguments, it is unlikely that the courts would sanction such a major operation upon a young man incapable of consenting to it himself.

My patient, Sophie, is 14 and has suffered from anorexia nervosa for the past two years. She is currently refusing all food. We, the medical team, along with her parents feel that she should now receive nasogastric feeds. Can I begin compulsory feeding or do I need the court's permission?

The law allows feeding of patients suffering from anorexia nervosa as part of the treatment of their mental disorder. Although the courts have not asked that cases are referred to them, it would be advisable to discuss the case with your local NHS Trust legal advisor before feeding is commenced.

Mr Syms is currently detained under Section 3 of the MHA and suffers from schizophrenia. He has a large inguinal hernia and the surgical team are keen to repair it so that there is no risk of strangulation later. Mr Syms refuses to consent to the operation. Can we proceed anyway, as we feel the operation is in his best interests?

If Mr Syms is mentally competent, he may lawfully refuse the operation. In this case there is nothing you can do, regardless of what you regard his best interests to be.

If he is incompetent – and not likely to regain competence with treatment – you may act in his best interests (which may include proceeding with the operation on his inguinal hernia).

References

1   Riverside Mental Health NHS Trust v Fox (1993) **20** *BMLR*: 1.

2   Re F (mental patient: sterilisation) (1990) **2** *AC*: 1, sub nom F v West Berkshire Health Authority (1989) **2** *All ER*: 545.

CHAPTER 6

Life and death, dying and killing

Victoria Tippett

Dying is a very important time in people's lives and needs handling with sensitivity. When the process goes well, a person's last weeks can be a time for personal growth and allow for reconciliation within a family. However, when it is badly handled, the suffering of the patient and their family can be compounded.

Palliative care involves the care of terminally ill patients. It aims to make the patient's death as painless, dignified and humane as possible. Within the specialty are both advocates and opponents of euthanasia. Broadly speaking, the advocates argue that given their role in making death as painless and acceptable to the patient as possible, in some cases the best way to achieve this would be to help the patient die at a time of their own choosing. The opponents counter that euthanasia runs contrary to the aims of palliative care – and is effectively giving up on what can be a very rewarding final period of a person's life. They argue that palliative care works to ensure that even the end of a patient's life is worthwhile, and euthanasia would undermine that and hence the work of palliative care as a whole. The arguments are much more subtle than this and will be explored in detail below. However, it is against this background that the ethical debate is played out.

It is important at the chapter's outset to define some of the key terms that will be used.

- **Voluntary euthanasia**: where a doctor ends a patient's life at his or her request.
- **Physician-assisted suicide**: where a doctor provides a patient with the means to commit suicide.
- **Life-prolonging treatment**: all treatment which has the potential to postpone the patient's death and includes cardiopulmonary resuscitation (CPR), artificial ventilation, specialised treatments such as chemotherapy or dialysis, antibiotics and artificial nutrition and hydration.
- **Basic care**: all the steps essential to keep a patient comfortable – warmth, shelter, pain relief, the management of distressing symptoms such as vomiting or breathlessness and the offer of oral hydration and nutrition.

The arguments about the ethics of actions taken towards the end of a person's life rage on, and this chapter contains just a summary of the salient points. First, it examines in turn the doctrine of double effect, killing and letting die, ordinary and extraordinary means. It will explain the law as it stands with regard to withholding/withdrawal of treatment, euthanasia and assisted suicide. Finally, the process of drawing up do not resuscitate (DNR) orders and advance directives, and their legal status, will be explained. This chapter should help individuals to identify which ethical arguments they feel are right and hence guide their practice in areas of the law which remain grey, as well as clearly stating the doctor's legal position where it is well defined.

The doctrine of double effect

The doctrine of double effect rests on the principle that an action intended to result in good can be carried out even though that good result can only be achieved at the expense of a coincident bad effect. It is a balance in which the good result is seen to outweigh the bad effect – a form of moral mathematics in which the deduction of a small amount of bad still leaves a net gain of good. This doctrine has support in religious quarters – particularly amongst Roman Catholic followers.

According to the doctrine of double effect, it would be acceptable to administer doses of morphine to a terminally ill man to relieve him of excruciating pain, despite knowing that the dose of morphine given will shorten the man's life. However, it would not be acceptable to administer the same dose of morphine to another man in just as much pain but who is expected to make a full recovery from his illness. In the former case the shortening of the man's life is a coincidental bad effect, and the good effect outweighs the bad, but in the latter the bad effect is so significant that it cannot be outweighed by the good.

Some opponents of the doctrine of double effect argue that death is the worst of all evils and so anything that involves shortening life cannot also be good. Others argue that the doctrine of double effect is simply splitting hairs and that knowingly shortening the patient's life is the same as hastening their death, and can be equated with euthanasia.

Many palliative care specialists argue that proper use of the analgesic ladder allows appropriate pain control to be achieved without any hastening of death.

Killing and letting die

The essence of the argument for a distinction between killing and letting die is that one is culpable for killing as it involves an action, but that in letting die no action is involved – just inaction – and so nobody is culpable.

Opponents of this view argue that it is the end result that is important – death of the patient. Given this, the means by which that is achieved – action or in-action – do not matter. If it is wrong to kill then by extension it is wrong to let someone die.

Ordinary and extraordinary means

The distinction between ordinary and extraordinary means has been supported by doctors and lawyers. It states that a doctor is under no moral (or legal) obli-gation to resort to extraordinary methods to prolong their patient's life. This distinction features strongly in Roman Catholic teaching.

In 1957 Pope Pius XII stated:

'Man has a right and a duty in cases of severe illness to take the necessary steps to preserve life and health . . . But he is obliged at all times to employ only ordinary means . . . that is to say those means which do not impose an extraordinary burden on himself or others.'

Or, as another unknown source said:

'One must not kill, but needst not strive officiously to keep alive.'

Opponents of this view argue that the distinction between ordinary and extra-ordinary means is arbitrarily drawn and subjective in its definition, creating an artificial distinction to allow euthanasia in through the back door in cer-tain cases.

Withholding treatment

This area of both ethics and law is a difficult one for doctors to examine, as it involves situations in which they have to admit that their further efforts would be futile. It involves primarily neonates born with physical or mental abnormal-ities but who could, with medical support, survive. In these situations the ques-tion examined is whether it is more humane to allow 'nature to take its course' and to offer no medical support, so that the neonate dies and does not endure a life of suffering, or whether all life is, irrespective of suffering, precious and therefore always preferable to death. The arguments of killing and letting die (described above) also play a part, with opponents of withholding treatment arguing that such 'letting die' is morally equivalent to killing the neonate and so unjustifiable.

Cases of this nature have come to court. In general the law tends to follow the doctor's lead and support their clinical autonomy. It is the doctor's assessment of the futility or otherwise of treatment, with the decision focused on the neonate's 'best interests', which guides the court's decisions.

> '... I can conceive of no situation where it would be proper ... to order a doctor, whether directly or indirectly, to treat a child in the manner contrary to his or her clinical judgment. I would go further. I find it difficult to conceive of a situation where it would be a proper exercise of the jurisdiction to make an order positively requiring a doctor to adopt a particular course of treatment in relation to a child.'[1]

Withdrawal of treatment

This area is principally involved in the ethics and law of withdrawing supportive treatment from patients in a persistent vegetative state (PVS). Again, it is a difficult area for doctors to address, as it involves them admitting failure and the futility of their further efforts.

The key legal case in this area is *Airedale NHS Trust v Bland* (1993) 1 *All ER*: 821. It involved a young man who had been injured in a football stadium disaster and was left in a PVS. His family felt that it was in his best interests for treatment to be withdrawn and for him to be allowed to die. In this case it was clearly distinguished that withdrawal of treatment does not constitute euthanasia.

> 'This is not a case about euthanasia because it does not involve any external agency of death. It is about whether, and how, the patient should be allowed to die.'[2]

The legal position is that if a diagnosis has been made that a patient is in a PVS and it is deemed that it is the patient's best interests to allow them to die, then doctors may withdraw treatment of that patient.

The legal argument for this was made as follows:

1   treatment of the incompetent is governed by necessity and necessity is, in turn, defined in terms of the patient's best interests
2   once there is no hope of recovery, any interest in being kept alive disappears and, with it, the justification for invasive therapy also disappears
3   in the absence of necessity, there can be no duty to act and, in the absence of a duty, there can be no criminality in an omission.

It is important that a PVS has been accurately diagnosed. The distinguishing features include an irregular circadian sleep–wake cycle unaccompanied by any behaviour expressing self-awareness, recognition of external stimuli or consistent evidence of attention, inattention or learned responses that has been present for at least a year.

Euthanasia

Euthanasia has many definitions, but can be summarised as the premature ending of a life with the intention to relieve suffering. It may be further subdivided into active or passive euthanasia. Active euthanasia or 'mercy killing' is ending a patient's life by some active means such as administering a rapidly lethal injection. Passive euthanasia is where life in shortened by not carrying out an action, for example not giving antibiotics to a patient with a terminal illness who is suffering from a bacterial pneumonia.

The ethical arguments for and against euthanasia are lengthy, and those described below are simply a thumbnail sketch of each case.

Pro-euthanasia

Euthanasia is the embodiment of the principles of autonomy, choice and human rights. If euthanasia is legalised, people are given choice. In a pluralistic society, people disagree about what kind of death they find meaningful.

> '... what sort of death is right for a particular person gives the best meaning to that person's life ... for those people who felt that to be kept alive in a situation which they found unacceptable would be harmful to their lives as a whole, cheapening what they had valued.'[3]

The sanctity of life principle, argued for by many religious groups (see below), is not shared by all and it is hurtful for someone who does not believe in a deity, for example the Christian God, to be expected to suffer intolerable pain or indignity in deference to God. It is not appropriate to base the law upon religious doctrines shared by only a minority of society's members.

> 'Having created the situation in which lives are routinely saved, transformed or prolonged by medical intervention, we can hardly pretend that the process of dying, and that alone, must be left to nature.'[4]

Advances in medical techniques have meant that:

> '... the dominant fear today is of being denied release from a prolonged period of painful, distressing and undignified dying.'[5]

Even if not everyone took the option of euthanasia, the knowledge that it was available as a last resort would be a comfort to those in fear of the future. It may also more readily allow patients who choose to die at home to do so, rather than having to die in an institution.

Anti-euthanasia

'We live in a society that is more than just a group of individuals'[6] and the rights of the individual are to be balanced by their social responsibilities. Whilst euthanasia grants the rights of some individuals, it is at an unacceptable cost to other, more vulnerable members of society. To grant the rights of some yet not others runs contrary to the principle of justice. Euthanasia would limit the autonomy of doctors, who should not be put in a position where patients could demand their collaboration in bringing about the patient's death. A '... licence for euthanasia would quickly become a duty for health-care workers to take part in it ...'[7]

The religious argument is that human life is a gift from God and so should be preserved and cherished, and that the gift is to be given and taken only at God's will – not that of a human being.

The role of killer does not sit well with that of healer and life-saver more traditionally associated with medical practice. The British Medical Association (BMA) states that:

> '... if doctors are authorised to kill or help kill, however carefully circumscribed the situation, they acquire an additional role, alien to the traditional one of healer. Their relationship with all their patients is perceived as having changed and as a result some may come to fear the doctor's visit.'[8]

Euthanasia would be the first step on a slippery slope towards active termination of life for those deemed worthless by society. Compare euthanasia with the legalisation of abortion. The number of abortions performed each year far exceeds the predictions made before the Abortion Act was passed, and what was intended as permission for doctors to perform abortions in certain circumstances is now an expectation of abortion on demand. It is reasonable to fear that society would slip towards cases where doctors perceive death is in the patient's best interests, even where no request for euthanasia has been made. The response to those requesting euthanasia should instead be to help them to regain a sense of self-worth and not to collude with their despair. The BMA notes that '... if handled well, the crisis of impending death can be a time of personal growth and reconciliation for all those close to the dying person'.[9]

Assisted suicide

Suicide itself is not illegal, but assisting a person to commit suicide is a crime and can result in a prison sentence of up to 14 years' duration. Doctors are not exempt from this, and the law views them no differently from anyone else assisting a person to commit suicide. Diane Pretty, a patient suffering from motor neurone disease, recently challenged this in the European Court of Human Rights, asking that her husband be immune from prosecution if he helped her to commit suicide. The court found that the UK law rendering assisted suicide illegal did not infringe Mrs Pretty's human rights.

The law

Euthanasia is illegal. Any intentional killing – even at a patient's request – is a criminal offence. It carries a mandatory life sentence. As stated above, although suicide is legal, assisted suicide is not.

Advance directives

An advance directive sets out a patient's wishes with regard to their medical treatment if they were to become incompetent to consent or refuse interventions. It may be particularly useful when a patient is suffering from a progressive illness. If they know that they will become incompetent they can set out their wishes in writing before that time arises. Advance directives allow a right to express choices, but not a right to demand treatment. If the healthcare team looking after a patient deems that further treatment is futile and not in the patient's best interests, any advance directive they may have made requesting all possible treatment will have no legal force and will be disregarded. However, adults can, if competent at the time of making the decision, make an advance refusal of medical treatment.

> '... it has been held that a patient of sound mind may, if properly informed, require that life support should be discontinued. The same principle applies where the patient's refusal to give his consent has been expressed at an earlier date, before he became unconscious or otherwise incapable of communicating it.'[10]

A patient can change their mind at any time, and more recent choices made by a competent patient can override a previously written advance directive. It is important to remember that advance directives are not covered by legislation, although common law recognises that advance refusal of treatment has legal force. In any case where an advance directive conflicts with an existing statute, the directive is disregarded.

DNR orders

It is possible to attempt to perform CPR on any person whose respiratory and cardiac function fails. As these failures are an unavoidable part of the dying process, CPR can theoretically be performed upon any individual before they die. However, for some patients, cardiopulmonary arrest is just the last stage of their illness and CPR would be inappropriate. In these circumstances the traumatic process of attempting CPR would be undignified and ineffective, and can be prevented by the creation of a DNR order. Where the patient is competent, this must always be sensitively discussed with the patient and not drawn up without their informed consent.

The guidelines drawn up by the Royal College of Nursing (RCN) and Resuscitation Council (UK) are as follows.

1   It is agreed that CPR should be routinely undertaken in all patients who suffer cardiac or respiratory arrest except:

   • where the patient's condition indicates that effective CPR is unlikely to be successful
   • where this is not in accord with the recorded, sustained wishes of the patient who is mentally competent
   • where successful CPR is likely to be followed by a length and quality of life which would not be acceptable to the patient.

2   The overall responsibility for DNR decisions rests with the consultant in charge of the patient's care. This decision should be made after appropriate consultation and consideration of all aspects of the patient's condition. The perspective of other members of the medical and nursing team, the patient and, with due regard to patient confidentiality, the patient's relatives or close friends, may all be valuable in helping to reach a decision.

3   Sensitive exploration of the patient's wishes should be undertaken. This should ideally be carried out by the consultant concerned in some circumstances, for example when a patient is at risk of cardiac or respiratory failure or has a terminal illness. Such discussions should be documented in the patient's record.

Transplantation

Transplantation is the removal of tissue from one site and its replacement in another. There are three main forms that transplantation can take.

1 Autotransplantation: taking tissue from one part of a person and using it to treat another part of that individual. Examples include iliac crest bone grafts or split skin grafts. Generally this poses no ethical or legal dilemmas and is not further discussed in this chapter.
2 Xenotransplantation (heterotransplantation): transplantation of tissue from a member of one species to a member of another. For example, the transplantation of a pig heart valve to a human patient.
3 Homotransplantation: this involves allografts – transplantation of tissue from one human to another human. For example, the transplantation of a mother's left kidney to her son.

Both homotransplantation and xenotransplantation pose complex ethical dilemmas which are reflected in the difficulties that the law has in addressing these issues. This chapter will explore each in turn.

Xenotransplantation

Xenotransplantation is still largely experimental. One of its key difficulties is the large amount of immunosuppression needed so that the patient's body does not reject the donor tissue.

As xenotransplantation is still in the developmental phase, many of the ethical problems it poses are theoretical. There are three main strands of argument. The first concerns the potential threat to the community of viruses currently affecting only animals, but that could cross the species barrier via xenotransplantation. The second is questioning whether it is morally defensible to use animals as organ donors, producing creatures just to fulfil our own needs. The third concerns a vague feeling that many people have that it is 'unnatural' to have an animal organ inside them. This is particularly true in the case of heart transplantation – an already emotive area given the widespread lay belief that the heart makes the individual unique and is spiritually significant.

The UK government has established the Xenotransplantation Interim Regulatory Authority to oversee how xenotransplantation develops. More information is available at http://www.doh.gov.uk/ukxira/

Homotransplantation

Homotransplantation is part of normal clinical practice within the UK. For transplants to be safely carried out the organs and tissues for transplantation must be disease free. Their removal should not cause harm to the donor, so living donors will only be able to give up tissues that can be replaced or, occasionally, a solid organ of which they have reserve function. For example, one kidney may be donated, provided that the donor's remaining kidney works well. All other donations must come from cadavers or 'beating heart' donors.

Living donors

If the organ or tissue in question can be easily replaced by the body, such as blood or bone marrow, there are two relevant issues. Firstly, the pain the donor endures whilst the tissue is harvested, and whether they should be financially compensated for this. Secondly, the allied commercial aspect of donation, and the prevention of undue pressure being placed upon donors if money were used as an inducement to participate.

In UK law, no person is allowed to consent to their being killed or seriously injured. New technology allows us to use *part* of certain organs, such as lobes of lung or sections of liver, whilst not compromising the overall function of the donor. However, the donation of certain vital organs such as the heart and brain is prohibited (*see* 'domino transplant' below for a potential exception).

It has been established in common law that live organ donation may be carried out so long as there is informed consent on the part of the donor to a surgical operation which is, for them, not therapeutic. Statutory regulation was also set out in the Organ Transplants Act 1989. Section 2 of the Act made it illegal for any live organ transplant to occur between persons not related (genetically) without the agreement of the Unrelated Live Transplant Regulatory Authority. However, it is interesting to note that transplantation between those who are genetically related is not subject to statutory control. The definition of genetic relationship can be found in Section 2(2) of the Act. The Organ Transplants Act 1989 is due to be repealed and replaced with the Human Tissue Bill, drafted following the Retained Organs Commission. Further details of this Bill (at the time of writing not yet law) can be found in Chapter 9.

The requirements of the Unrelated Live Transplant Regulatory Authority are stringent. They include an absence of any monetary involvement (except payment of legitimate expenses), counselling of both the donor and the patient and the requirement that the donor must understand the process involved. If the transplant is part of a domino transplant – for example where a young adult with cystic fibrosis has damaged lungs and receives a heart–lung transplant via cadaveric donation, but then can donate their healthy heart to another recipient – the Authority insists only on the non-payment of the donor. Its other requirements do not apply in this case.

Donation by children

Although the legality and morality of donation by adults, both related and unrelated, are clear, the area of donation by children remains problematic. It is relatively common for children to be required to donate organs but UK courts have not officially decided whether operations for live organ donation carried out on children younger than 16 are legal. Therefore guidance can only be taken from the law on consent for therapeutic operations for minors (children under 16).

Usually, unless the child is 'Gillick competent', parental consent to treatment must be obtained for all minors. However, for such parental consent to be valid, the treatment should be in the child's best interests. This usually means that the child should derive benefit from the procedure.

In the case of live organ donation, is it reasonable to argue that the procedure benefits the child? Many such cases involve donation occurring between siblings. It has been argued by some commentators that there is therefore psychological benefit to the donor child in helping their sibling and uniting their family. However, with such potential for benefit comes the potential for harm as well. Children can come under undue pressure to donate in order to please their parents, who are likely to be very upset by the illness of their other child (the patient).

There is no UK case law involving minors as organ donors or any statute provision. Cases involving adults with learning difficulties that result in them having the mental age of a minor have come to court. In *Re Y (adult patient) (transplant: bone marrow)* (1997) 35 MLR 111, an adult with disabilities was allowed to donate bone marrow to their sibling suffering from lymphoma. It was argued that without this treatment the child with lymphoma would require more care from its mother, leaving her less time to devote to the donor adult's needs. Therefore the donation was found to be in the disabled adult's best interests.

The UK legal system does not prohibit child live organ donation, but the World Health Organization has called for a complete ban on the use of minors as organ donors. In Australia such a ban exists on all donations of non-regenerative tissue by minors.

Donation by patients who are in a persistent vegetative state (PVS)

It is not acceptable to use the organs or tissues of patients who are in a PVS and therefore not yet dead. It is equally unacceptable to hasten the death of such patients so that their organs may be available for donation sooner. This is reinforced in the BMA's 'Guidelines Relating to the Persistent Vegetative State'.

'Beating heart' donors

Often organs for donation are obtained from patients who have been on ventilatory and/or cardiovascular support systems but who are diagnosed as being brain dead. These patients, once a diagnosis of brain death has been made, may continue to receive ventilatory and cardiovascular support to allow the maintenance of viable organs for donation during the transplant operation. This is where the term 'beating heart' donor comes from. Whilst a difficult situation for both the relatives and clinicians involved, the potential benefits are enormous and a large proportion of high-quality organs may be harvested in this way.

Cadaveric donors

The Human Tissue Act 1961 regulates the use of tissues and organs from the deceased. Although the Act is being revised, no alterations have yet been passed as law, so it is the original Act that is discussed here. If the deceased has made a specific request during life (often via the donor card system) for organ removal after death then such donation is lawful. The tissue may be for use in the therapeutic setting and given to a patient, research setting and used for experimentation, or educational setting and used for medical school dissection classes. If the deceased did not request organ donation, but the person who lawfully possesses the body* has no reason to believe the deceased objected to organ donation, and the surviving spouse or any surviving relative of the deceased does not object then they may proceed with donation.

Although according to the letter of the law it is possible for a doctor to act upon the consent of the deceased to donate, despite the wishes of their living relatives that the body is not touched, in practice this is very rare. Of note, the coroner can veto organ retrieval if the deceased comes within their jurisdiction and it would adversely affect their enquiries if organs were to be removed.

Neonatal donors

The major area of interest in neonatal donation has been the use of anencephalic infants as donors. The Medical Royal Colleges of the UK have stated that 'organs for transplantation can be removed from anencephalic infants when

---

* Some debate exists as to who the Act means by the person who lawfully possesses the body. It is currently felt that this refers to the hospital administrative officer who has physical possession of the body, and not the executors of the deceased's will.

two doctors who are not members of the transplant team agree that spontaneous respiration has ceased'.[11]

How do we get enough organs to meet the demand?

At present, healthy members of society *opt in* to the organ donation scheme, usually by carrying a donor card and notifying their nearest relatives of their wishes. It has been suggested that an *opt out* system would be more effective and result in more organs being available without overriding the wishes of the deceased or surviving relatives. This is in concordance with the ethical view that it is morally wrong for so many potentially available organs to go to waste whilst patients waiting for transplants continue to suffer. In some European countries such a system already exists. In general, the system works as follows. All citizens are presumed to consent to the removal of their organs after death for donation. If a person objects to this they can register their refusal with a national body and their organs will not be used after their death. Also, if their next of kin vetoes the donation once death has occurred, this refusal is respected. Such a system is a long way from the current UK position and political parties have for some time seemed reluctant to change the status quo, despite the growing waiting lists for organ transplantation.

The alternative and less controversial proposed method for increasing the level of organ donation is to encourage clinicians involved in patient care at the end of life to ask about organ donation. Whilst trained specialists in this field will be available to lead such discussions in some cases, for the majority it will be up to the normal clinical team to broach this difficult subject. However, an ethical duty rests upon all of us to attempt to maximise the number of organs available, whilst remaining sensitive to the individual needs of patients or relatives that we see before us.

 # Where you stand

- Euthanasia is illegal.
- Assisted suicide is illegal.
- Advance directives that refuse treatment have legal force under common law but are not covered by statute.
- Advance directives that express choices but do not refuse certain treatments are useful as evidence of a patient's preferences but can be superseded by

any subsequent statements by the patient, and have no legal force in their own right.

- The responsibility for DNR orders lies with the consultant in charge of a patient's care. The decision should be made after appropriate consultation with the healthcare team, the patient and (where appropriate) the patient's relatives and close friends.
- Organ donation by a living donor is legal if they give informed consent to the surgical procedure which is, for them, non-therapeutic.
- 'Beating heart' donation is legal once the patient has been diagnosed as being brain dead.
- Cadaveric donation is lawful if, during life, the patient made a specific request for their organs to be removed after death.
- Cadaveric donation does not always require the donor's consent during life if those in legal possession of the body and the spouse or nearest relatives are in agreement that the patient would not have opposed organ donation.

 # Where you fall

- Euthanasia is a criminal offence and carries a mandatory life sentence.
- Assisted suicide carries a maximum sentence of 14 years.
- The donation of vital organs by a living donor is prohibited.
- Donation by persons not genetically related may not proceed unless you have the agreement of the Unrelated Live Transplant Regulatory Authority.
- It is not acceptable to use organs or tissues of patients in a PVS or to hasten the death of such patients in order to facilitate organ donation.

Cases

Mr Blake is 50 years old and suffers from muscular dystrophy. He was first diagnosed with the condition when he was 45. He was very worried by his diagnosis, and searched for more information about it on the internet. As he learnt how he was likely to die, he made an advance directive, stating that he would like to receive full medical care including artificial ventilation or circulatory support when he was in the terminal stages of his illness. Over the past five years Mr Blake has become progressively more ill. It is likely that he has only weeks to live. He now struggles to breathe and his wife is keen that he should receive artificial ventilation, but we the medical team caring for him feel that such treatment would be futile and not in Mr Blake's best interests. Mrs Blake produces the advance directive that her husband drew up and says that this supports her case for providing him with artificial ventilation.

What should we, the medical team, do?

Whilst advance directives refusing treatment have legal force under common law, advance directives requesting treatment do not. The decision rests with you as the medical team caring for Mr Blake. If you feel that artificial ventilation would be futile and not in Mr Blake's best interests then you have no legal duty to follow his directive. Your clinical decision not to provide artificial ventilation would be supported by the law.

I am a GP, and Mrs Jones has been my patient for the last 30 years. Mrs Jones suffers from Huntington's disease. She is grossly disabled, but mentally competent. She has expressed her desire to die to me many times over the last two years. I have attempted to talk to her about this and offered her help with what I see as reactive depression related to her illness, but she remains adamant that death is her only way out. She states that she will commit suicide, but cannot leave her house and so cannot acquire the means to do so. She has asked me to help in the only way left – to get her a drug she could inject and kill herself with. She says it is the only way I can ease her pain. She has reassured me that I will not be at fault – she will be killing herself.

What do I do?

To go along with Mrs Jones' plan and to provide her with the means to commit suicide would be a criminal offence – assisted suicide – with a maximum sentence of 14 years' imprisonment. You cannot do this, but you can help Mrs Jones to cope with her symptoms via medication, pain control, psychological support and liaising with social services to ensure Mrs Jones has suitable carer provision.

Miss Smith suffers from multiple sclerosis. Her symptoms are well controlled most of the time, but occasionally she has severe relapses and requires hospitalisation. During her current admission, she asked me as the consultant in charge of her care if she could make a DNR order. She stated that in the event of her heart stopping, she would not want someone jumping up and down on her to try to restart it. Miss Smith is mentally competent, but not terminally ill.

What should I do?

Any mentally competent adult may refuse medical treatment, and CPR is no exception to this. Under common law, Miss Smith's advance refusal would be accepted. Although the overall responsibility for DNR orders rests with you, the consultant, you are legally obliged to accept Miss Smith's advance refusal, however absurd you may feel it is, and regardless of whether or not CPR is treatment which is likely to be needed in the near future.

> I am a Senior House Officer in anaesthetics working in the Intensive Treatment Unit (ITU). A patient of mine has been diagnosed as brain dead after a massive intracerebral haemorrhage. My consultant has asked me to talk to her family about organ donation. How do I do this?

It is important that you have senior support when undertaking such a task. A discussion of this nature should be conducted in a quiet, private room. Where possible you should give your pager or bleep to a colleague.

A good starting place is to discuss with the relatives their understanding of the patient's condition – both diagnosis and prognosis. It is important to explain that a diagnosis of brain death means the patient will not recover.

The next task is to discuss the patient's views on organ donation. Did they ever discuss this during their life? Did they carry a donor card? The family may have specific questions about how donation happens. If you cannot answer their questions offer to get back to them with answers once you have sought senior advice.

Although you should not coerce relatives into giving their consent, you have a duty to all the patients currently waiting for organ transplants to explain the positive benefits of organ donation and the number of lives that such operations may save. Examples of actual uses may be helpful, such as kidney transplants for patients on dialysis or corneal transplants to restore patients' sight.

It should be possible to give the relatives time to take in the information you have given them, get back to you with any questions they may think of and consider the options before giving you a decision. Time for such decisions may be limited due to ongoing damage to organs or pressure on ITU beds, but where possible relatives should not be rushed into making hasty decisions at what is a difficult time for them.

References

1   Re J (*a minor*) (1992) **4** *All ER*: 614.

2   Airedale NHS Trust v Bland (1993) **1** *All ER*: 821: 856.

3   Professor Dworkin @ http://www.bma.org.uk/ap.nsf/Content/pas+project+-+select+ctteereports

4   Voluntary Euthanasia Society @ http://www.bma.org.uk/ap.nsf/Content/pas+project+-+select+select+ctteereports

5   Mr Ludovic Kennedy @ http://www.bma.org.uk/ap.nsf/Content/pas+project+-+select+
    ctteereports

6   HOPE @ http://www.bma.org.uk/ap.nsf/Content/pas+project+-+select+ctteereports

7   SPUC @ http://www.bma.org.uk/ap.nsf/Content/pas+project+-+select+ctteereports

8   http://www.bma.org.uk/ap.nsf/Content/pas+project+-+select+ctteereports

9   http://www.bma.org.uk/ap.nsf/Content/pas+project+-+select+ctteereports

10 Airedale NHS Trust v Bland (1993) 1 *All ER*: 821.

11 Report of the Working Party of the Conference of Medical Royal Colleges and their Facul-
    ties in the United Kingdom on Organ Transplantation in Neonates (1988).

CHAPTER 7

Human reproduction

Victoria Tippett and Louise Ma

The birth of children is a necessary part of the continuation of human life. For most couples, conceiving a child is no problem, but up to 1 in 6 will experience infertility. This is in stark contrast with those who either wish to render themselves infertile via sterilisation or who wish to terminate a pregnancy they have conceived.

Many view the ability to procreate as an automatic or 'God-given' right, and this is acknowledged in the Human Rights Act 1998. Article 8 covers the right to respect for private and family life, and Article 12 the right to marry and found a family. For every right there is a corresponding duty that falls upon someone else. In the case of reproductive rights that someone is usually a member of the health service. The result is that much of the work in medical ethics and law is focused on reproductive health and some of the issues involved are far from simple.

This chapter will describe the main topics and focus upon the legal issues. The areas covered are the legal status of the embryo and fetus, the legal relationship between mother and fetus, prenatal screening and claims of 'wrongful life', assisted conception and the Human Fertilisation and Embryology Act 1990, the Abortion Act 1967 and sterilisation.

The legal status of the embryo and fetus

There are several medical terms used to describe a developing child *in utero* from its conception to its birth. They have strict temporal definitions, such as an embryo – the child from day 14 after conception until it has implanted into the endometrium. These lines of demarcation start to become blurred when we attempt to decide at what point a fetus becomes a person, and when it should be accorded rights.

Individuals disagree and often it is religious groups who voice the strongest opinions when defining the point at which life begins. The Catholic Church believes that a person is created at the moment of conception and should be accorded rights from then onwards. The Jewish faith holds that a person is created at the time when pregnancy is recognisable (a time which varies from mother to mother). The Christian faith embraces a broad spectrum of opinion, from the position of the Catholic Church to one in which the fetus only has rights once it is sufficiently developed to be able to exist independently outside of the womb. Pro-Life campaigners who wish to afford full rights to fetuses usually refer to them as unborn children, whereas Pro-Choice campaigners who advocate maternal choice often use the term fetus.

Despite such a vast spectrum of opinion, the law strictly defines the point at which a fetus acquires rights as the time when the fetus is **born alive**. A neonate must survive for 48 hours (to prove that they were viable) before any damages can be recovered from negligence in their care.

This definition means that nobody – not even the father of the fetus – can prevent its mother from procuring an abortion. Although this denies the father any rights until the moment of birth, it respects the mother's rights to bodily integrity and autonomy. It is an unhappy compromise but, as yet, no better solution has been found.

The legal relationship between mother and fetus

A mother has no duty to her unborn child until the moment of its birth. She may choose to put the health and life of her fetus at risk by undertaking any activity she wishes (such as smoking, drinking excess alcohol or abusing drugs). So long as she is competent she may also refuse treatment, even if such a refusal will affect her fetus. No civil action may be taken on behalf of the fetus if the negligent behaviour of its mother caused its death except in one case. If the fetus is injured or killed during a road traffic accident, its mother can be held accountable. This exception is justified on the grounds that insurance available to the mother can settle such claims. In all other cases it is felt that to admit cases brought by a child against its mother would compromise the parent–child relationship and may be used as a weapon in matrimonial disputes.

It is only the mother who has no duty to her unborn child. Third parties (including the father of the fetus) who attack the woman carrying the fetus may be held liable for the manslaughter or murder of that fetus, even if the woman herself survives the attack.

Consent to caesarean section

The position described above, of a mother's right to choose until the time of her child's birth, has been challenged several times when her refusal to consent to a caesarean section has entailed putting the fetus' life at risk. In the vast majority of UK cases so far, the courts have found the mother incompetent to consent or refuse the operation and have ruled that she should have the caesarean section performed in her best interests. However, the legal position states that:

'1   every person was presumed to have the capacity to consent to or to refuse medical treatment unless or until that presumption was rebutted

2   a competent woman who had the capacity to decide might, for religious or other reasons whether rational or irrational or for no reason at all, choose not to have medical intervention even though the consequence might be the death or serious handicap of the child or her own death. In that event the court did not have jurisdiction to declare medical intervention and the question of her own best interests, objectively, did not arise

3   irrationality connoted a decision which was so outrageous in its defiance of logic or of accepted moral standards that no sensible person who had applied his mind to the question to be decided could have arrived at it. Although it might be thought that irrationality sat uneasily with competence to decide, panic, indecisiveness and irrationality in themselves did not as such amount to incompetence but might be symptoms or evidence of incompetence. The graver the consequences of the decision, the commensurately greater the level of competence was required to take the decision.'

And also:

'Temporary factors such as confusion, shock, fatigue, pain or drugs might completely erode capacity but only if such factors were operating to such a degree that the ability to decide was absent.'[1]

This means that factors often present during labour, such as pain, fear and shock, would not ordinarily render a woman incompetent to consent to or refuse an operation if necessary. However, factors such as these may, in a few cases, combine to render her completely unable to make decisions and give her informed consent. In such a situation it is wise for the obstetrician involved to apply to the courts for a ruling to allow them to proceed with the operation. In these circumstances a ruling may be delivered remarkably quickly, as the situation requires swift choices to be made.

Prenatal screening and 'wrongful life'

Prenatal screening involves the performance of tests upon the mother and, in some cases, her fetus to attempt to detect genetic and developmental abnormalities. These may include blood tests, ultrasound scans and amniocentesis or chorionic villus sampling.

Although often thought of as a way to find 'defective' unborn children so that their mother can choose to abort the pregnancy, this is not always the case. Prenatal screening also allows parents-to-be to adjust, both emotionally and practically, to the arrival of a child with special needs. It may also allow the use of medical intervention, either prenatally, at delivery or in the immediate postnatal period, to alleviate the child's suffering or correct a physical defect. For example, if a diaphragmatic hernia was detected on ultrasound scan prenatally, arrangements could be made for the baby to be delivered by caesarean section at a specialist centre with paediatric surgeons on hand to repair the physical defect immediately.

With prenatal testing comes the risk of error. This includes personal error on the part of the interpreter of the result, or the ultrasonographer, and laboratory error in terms of the misreading of sample results by equipment. No screening test is 100% sensitive and it is often difficult to explain this to parents. Errors in this area may lead to false reassurance of parents that their fetus is healthy, and subsequent distress when they give birth to an abnormal baby, or (less commonly) the warning that a fetus is abnormal and the subsequent birth of a normal baby. Such errors have led to legal claims of 'wrongful life'.

A claim for 'wrongful life' is one in which the child alleges that through the negligence of the defendant (for example, an NHS Trust), its parents were not afforded the opportunity to choose an abortion whilst it was a fetus. The child is seeking damages for the impaired existence they are being unwillingly forced to lead, hence the term 'wrongful life'. Were it not for the defendant's negligence, they would not be alive and so not be suffering.

In a case of 'wrongful life' the negligence may occur before conception (e.g. negligent genetic counselling) or after conception (e.g. doctor fails to detect abnormality in the fetus whilst performing an ultrasound scan). Such actions have generally been unsuccessful in the UK, and this area is now covered by the Congenital Disabilities (Civil Liability) Act 1976. This Act seems to exclude children from having a right to bring a case in these circumstances. Some legal commentators have argued that the wording of the Act does not exclude 'wrongful life' actions, but no subsequent cases have been brought to challenge this.

The ethical arguments for and against allowing 'wrongful life' actions are fascinating but beyond the scope of this chapter. For more information consult a larger text, such as Beauchamp and Childress[2] and Mason et al.[3]

Assisted conception

In the UK approximately 1 in 6 couples is infertile. This may be primary infertility, where the couple have never conceived a child and neither partner has children from a previous relationship, or secondary infertility, where the couple have never conceived a child together, but one or both partners have conceived children in previous relationships. Assisted conception attempts to overcome these couples' problems and allow them to have children.

There are two groups of assisted conception techniques. The first involves the couple's own gametes (sperm and ova), and may include sperm washing or intracytoplasmic sperm injection (ICSI). The second involves a third party and is a wider group. The third party may donate ova or sperm or may 'lend' her womb to the couple so that their embryo can grow (a person referred to as a surrogate mother).

The ethics of assisted conception is a vast area and, for reasons of brevity, will only be mentioned here where it relates directly to the legal position.

The Human Fertilisation and Embryology Act 1990

Fertility treatment and assisted conception evolved as a specialty about 10 years before the creation of the Human Fertilisation and Embryology Act. As fertility treatment became more common and was carried out more widely, the public became concerned about its lack of regulation. The Act was created in 1990 and with it the Human Fertilisation and Embryology Authority (HFEA). The HFEA consists of 21 members appointed by the UK's health ministers, and over half its members have no medical or embryology background. The HFEA regulates all fertility treatment and embryo research occurring within the UK and enforces the requirements of the Human Fertilisation and Embryology Act. All fertility clinics require a licence from the HFEA before they can offer services to infertile couples.

The HFEA guidelines are extensive, but those referring to the selection of couples suitable to enter treatment programmes, selection of donors and the welfare of the child resulting from the fertility treatment are relevant. These are summarised below.

Donors

1   A donor may not contribute to more than 10 live births. A fertility centre should check whether a prospective donor has previously attended another clinic, to ensure that the 10 live birth limit is not exceeded.
2   Centres should ensure that the donor is fully aware of the tests that will be carried out on their donation, and that they may reveal previously unsuspected defects, such as genetic abnormalities or human immunodeficiency virus (HIV) infection.

3   Sperm donors should be under the age of 45. Egg donors should be under the age of 35.
4   People providing gametes for donation should be paid no more than £15 for each donation plus reasonable expenses. These are laid out in Section 12(e) of the Human Fertilisation and Embryology Act 1990.
5   When selecting donors, centres should pay particular attention to any history of heritable disorders, any personal history of transmissible infection, the level of potential fertility, whether the prospective donor has children of their own and their motivation for wanting to donate gametes.

Couples

1   Couples where the female partner is over 35 or the male partner is over 45 may only have gametes taken for their own use, and such couples should be offered clinical advice and counselling before deciding whether to proceed with treatment.
2   Only in exceptional circumstances should gametes be taken from those aged under 18, and the gametes should only be used for the treatment of that person or their partner. The centre must be satisfied that the person is capable of giving their informed consent to the procedure.
3   When deciding whether or not to offer treatment, the centre should consider the medical needs and wishes of the couple, and of any children who may be involved.
4   When deciding which couples to offer treatment to, a centre's policy should not be arbitrary or discriminatory.

Welfare of the child

1   A woman should not be provided with treatment unless the welfare of any child conceived as a result of the treatment (including the need for a father), and of any other child who may be affected by the birth has been considered. Centres should have a clear written policy for assessing the welfare of the child.
2   Couples or individuals seeking treatment are entitled to a sensitive, fair and unprejudiced assessment of their situation and needs.
3   Factors to consider include their desire for a child, ability to provide a stable and supportive environment, their health and age and the impact of these factors in their ability to meet the child's needs, their ability to cope with the implications of multiple births, any risk of harm to the child (due to neglect, heritable disorders, etc.) and the effect of a new baby upon existing children in the family.

4 Centres should take all reasonable steps to ascertain who will be legally responsible for the child created as a result of the treatment and who it is intended will raise them.
5 If donor gametes are used, the legal implications of this, the desire for the child to know about its genetic origin and possible family difficulties, especially if the donor is related to the receiving couple, should be considered.

Embryos

Only two embryos may be transferred in a single *in vitro* fertilisation (IVF) treatment cycle. Only in exceptional circumstances may three embryos be transferred, and the reasons for this should be clearly noted in the records.

Using donor gametes

Once a donor has consented to the use of their gametes they may make their donation. Sperm can be frozen for later thawing and use, but ova are not usually frozen due to poor outcomes after thawing and added risks of this method. Ova are usually fertilised immediately and the resulting embryos grown may then be used immediately for intrauterine insemination or frozen for later use.

Only the Assisted Reproduction and Gynaecology Centre is allowed to freeze ova. This facility is usually reserved for young women undergoing treatment (such as chemotherapy) that will render them infertile. It allows egg harvesting and storage to take place, so that when she has chosen a partner the woman's eggs may be thawed and fertilised. It is important to counsel such women that the success rate of using thawed ova is still low and there is no guarantee that future fertility treatment will be successful.

It is essential that before a person begins fertility treatment they have given their written informed consent. This must include specific details about the sperm or embryos' use, storage time and disposal. It is also important that they specify what should be done with their gametes or embryos should they die or become incapacitated at a later date.

It is illegal for sperm and embryos to be stored for more than 10 years.

If a woman becomes pregnant using donor sperm/donor eggs, she and her husband or partner (provided they sought fertility treatment together) will be acknowledged as the legal parents of the child when it is born.

The HFEA keeps a register of all children born as a result of fertility treatment. The HFEA respects donor anonymity at present.

Currently, once a person reaches 18 years of age or are over 16 but are about to marry, they can ask the HFEA whether they were born as a result of donor assisted conception. They should receive proper counselling before deciding whether to make such a request of the HFEA. The HFEA can tell them whether or not they are related to the person they wish to marry.

It was announced by the government in January 2004 that a change in the law is planned relating to donor anonymity. Children born as a result of ova or sperm donated after April 2005 will be able to access the identity of their donors when they are 18. This means that the first children will be able to request this in the year 2023. These regulations are not retrospective, so existing and previous donors' anonymity is respected.[4]

Using gametes of a dead spouse

If either partner is suffering from a terminal illness, they may consent to the removal and storage of their sperm or eggs so that their partner may use them to conceive children in the future. They must give their informed consent and must include with it specific instructions as to the storage, use and disposal of the gametes. The children created from such stored gametes will not be legally regarded as the children of the deceased parent.

The famous Diane Blood case of recent years was essentially different from the above. Sperm was taken from Mr Blood whilst he was in a coma, and thus unable to give his consent to its removal and storage. This was illegal but once done, Mrs Blood fought a legal battle to allow her to use the sperm in fertility treatment in the UK. She lost her case, but was eventually allowed to take the sperm abroad for use in fertility treatment there.

Pre-implantation genetic diagnosis

The development of pre-implantation genetic diagnosis (PIGD) during the 1980s allowed couples with genetic disease to have healthy children via IVF. Ova and sperm are taken from both potential parents and artificially fertilised in a laboratory. Then a cell from each fertilised embryo is taken for genetic analysis, looking for the genetic fingerprint of known diseases. Embryos 'free from disease' are then implanted into the female partner. The success rate for implantation after this procedure is approximately 25%.

The HFEA will only allow PIGD on medical grounds (e.g. family history of cystic fibrosis). They will not permit the screening of embryos to allow sex selection alone.

For the first time, in February 2002, the HFEA allowed a couple in the UK to use PIGD to select a child 'free from disease' with a suitable histocompatibility leucocyte antigen (HLA) match for their existing son, who suffers from thalassaemia. A Judicial Review in December 2002 challenged the ruling, but the original decision was upheld by the Court of Appeal in April 2003. The family are undergoing in vitro fertilisation treatment with PIGD to create a child whose stem cells could be donated to their existing son, Zain. The cells will be collected from its umbilical cord at birth, causing the infant no pain. They will then be used to try to save Zain's life.

This decision is controversial. Supporters argue that the use of PIGD here does not harm the newly created child, and actively benefits the elder brother, so there is benefit all round. To not make use of the available technology would have been to risk creating another baby with thalassaemia who would have suffered as much as the couple's first child. With PIGD such suffering is unnecessary. Opponents fear that the selection of some sorts of humans over others will lead down a slippery slope towards 'designer babies' and is reminiscent of Nazi eugenic programmes. They feel the new baby becomes a commodity and not a person.

Surrogacy

Surrogacy involves the carriage of a pregnancy by a woman on behalf of another woman or couple. It may be either partial surrogacy, where the surrogate's ovum is combined with donor sperm via intrauterine insemination, or complete surrogacy, where an already fertilised embryo is implanted into the surrogate's womb.

In the UK, a surrogate should voluntarily carry the couple's child. She may be paid expenses, but should not make financial gains from the arrangement. The Surrogacy Arrangements Act 1985 prevents surrogacy arrangements in the UK from being made on a commercial basis. This is in contrast with the USA, where a contract exists between the surrogate and the couple.

Under UK law, because the surrogate gives birth to the baby, she is regarded as its mother. The couple seeking fertility treatment must make a court order within six months of the child's birth. The child should be living with the couple at the time, they must both be over 18 years of age, and the child must be the product of one or both of the couple's gametes. If these criteria are not met, the couple must apply to adopt the child.

In some sad cases, the surrogate changes her mind before or shortly after giving birth to the child and refuses to give the baby to the couple. When such cases have gone to court they have always resulted in a ruling giving custody to the surrogate. The decisions have not discriminated between partial and complete surrogacy. Their reasoning is usually founded on the argument that during the pregnancy strong bonds have already been established between mother and child.

Abortion

The Abortion Act was passed in 1967 and was amended by the Human Fertilisation and Embryology Act in 1990. These two statutes afforded women greater control over their reproductive potential than had ever previously been the case. Before this time, when abortion was illegal, back street procedures were carried out by unqualified people and often resulted in potentially fatal complications for the young women. Mortality from abortions was vastly reduced by introduction of the 1967 Act.

The Abortion Act 1967 applies to England, Wales and Scotland. In Northern Ireland the Act has never been accepted and the abortion is illegal except under common law after a ruling in 1938. This allows abortion in exceptional circumstances involving risk to the woman's physical or mental health.

Conscientious objection

Under the Abortion Act 1967 medical practitioners may refuse to participate in abortions. These doctors should not be discriminated against, but nor should they discriminate against women seeking an abortion. Such doctors should make their views known to the patient and quickly refer them to another doctor who can deal with their request. Medical students may also conscientiously object to witnessing abortions, and should make their wishes known to the co-ordinator at the start of their training period.

The Abortion Act 1967 states that a registered medical practitioner may lawfully terminate a pregnancy, in an NHS hospital or on premises approved for this purpose, if two registered medical practitioners are of the opinion, formed in good faith, that:

1   the continuance of the pregnancy would involve risk to the life of the pregnant women greater than if the pregnancy were terminated
2   the termination is necessary to prevent grave permanent injury to the physical or mental health of the pregnant woman
3   the pregnancy has NOT exceeded its 24th week and that the continuance of the pregnancy would involve risk, greater than if the pregnancy were terminated, of injury to the physical or mental health of the pregnant woman
4   the pregnancy has NOT exceeded its 24th week and that the continuance of the pregnancy would involve risk, greater than if the pregnancy were terminated, of injury to the physical or mental health of the existing child(ren) of the family of the pregnant woman
5   there is substantial risk that if the child were born it would suffer from such physical or mental abnormalities as to be seriously handicapped

Emergency abortions

6   it was necessary to save the life of the woman
7   it was necessary to prevent grave permanent injury to the physical or mental health of the pregnant woman.

In the case of emergency abortions, the opinion of a second doctor is not required, and the restrictions on where the procedure may be carried out do not apply.

What constitutes a 'serious handicap' is not clear and is a matter of clinical judgement and accepted medical practice. In assessing the seriousness of the handicap it may be useful to consider:

- the probability of effective treatment either *in utero* or after birth
- the child's potential for self-awareness and ability to communicate with others
- the suffering that would be experienced by the child when born or by those caring for the child.

Preventing an abortion

The biological father of the fetus is not included in the Abortion Act. He has no rights to object to the abortion, nor can he force his partner to have an abortion against her will. The courts have upheld this and neither rights of the father nor rights of the child may be claimed until the baby is born.

Sterilisation

Sterilisation involves rendering a person permanently infertile. It may involve tubal ligation or a hysterectomy for a woman or a vasectomy for a man.

Sterilisation is not as ethically inert as it might at first seem. The Catholic Church opposes sterilisation and sees it as a mutilation of the human body and the deprivation of a natural function. Others object that an individual may later change their mind and be left with no option to restore their fertility. However, others see it as an individual giving their informed consent to an operation that allows them control over their fertility and thus reflects their autonomy.

Men

Men requesting a vasectomy must be adequately counselled before they are asked to consent to the operation. It is important that the method of the operation is explained, and it is clarified that the operation should be regarded as irreversible. It should be emphasised that there is a failure rate (of the order of 1–2 per 1000) and that another form of contraception should be used after the operation until two semen analyses have been carried out and found to be clear of sperm.

A case was brought against a surgeon alleging that he failed to warn a couple of the risk of the man's sterilisation being unsuccessful. When, two years later, his wife became pregnant, they sued for breach of contract. It was ruled that the surgeon had failed to warn them of this risk and the couple won the case.

Women

The above description of male sterilisation applies to female sterilisation too. It is vital that the risks are explained clearly. Tubal ligation is a less successful operation than a vasectomy, as well as involving more risk to the patient.

Cases of the sterilisation of mentally incompetent women involve the law on consent and competence, and have been discussed previously (Chapter 5).

Failed sterilisation and unwanted children

The birth of a child is usually a joyful event, but children born as a result of negligence are potential grounds for compensation. It is regarded that wrongful pregnancy is a personal injury and that it cannot be separated from its consequences, i.e. the birth of a child.

 # Where you stand

- The fetus has no rights until its birth.
- The mother has sole rights during pregnancy to consent to or refuse any intervention.
- Abortion is permitted after 24 weeks only if the life of the mother is at risk or if the fetus is at substantial risk of being severely mentally or physically handicapped.
- A doctor may refuse to be involved in abortions (and a medical student may refuse to witness them) but the doctor must refer the woman on to a colleague who will treat her.
- Pre-implantation genetic diagnosis may only be carried out for medical reasons.

- There is no legal agreement between a surrogate mother and the couple undergoing treatment – the surrogate is the legal mother.
- It is essential to counsel patients adequately about the risks and failure rate of sterilisation.
- Those donating gametes for their own use either during their lifetime or post-humously must give clear instructions about the use, storage and disposal of their gametes and any resulting embryos.

 # Where you fall

- All fertility centres must have a licence from the HFEA.
- No embryos may be stored for more than 10 years.
- Only in an emergency may one doctor authorise an abortion. At all other times two registered medical practitioners are required.
- Abortions that are not carried out in accordance with the Abortion Act 1967 are illegal and a criminal offence.
- If you fail to warn about the risk of failure of a sterilisation procedure, not only will you be found to be negligent but you may also be required to compensate the family for the birth of their unwanted child.

Cases

I am a GP and my patient, Miss Young, has come to me worried that she may be pregnant. A pregnancy test has come back positive and, according to her dates, she is eight weeks pregnant. She is unhappy and has asked me to refer her for an abortion. She states that she is too stressed at work and could not cope with a baby.

I do not object to abortion on religious grounds but I feel that Miss Young is not taking the decision seriously enough. I feel uncomfortable about signing her abortion form but what can I do?

Miss Young's request falls under point 3 on page 74 – the pregnancy has NOT exceeded its 24th week and that the continuance of the pregnancy would involve risk, greater than if the pregnancy were terminated, of injury to the physical or mental health of the pregnant woman.

Although her request is legal, you may conscientiously object to referring her for an abortion and signing her form for any personal reasons. You do not have to object on religious grounds. If you decide that you are not happy to sign her form, then you must explain this to Miss Young and refer her as soon as possible to a colleague who will not object to her request.

My consultant has asked me to consent Mr Walters for his vasectomy. Although I am aware of the risks of the surgery, what information should I give him about the risk of failure and the possibility of reversal at a later date?

You should emphasise to Mr Walters that sterilisation is intended to render him permanently infertile. If he were to change his mind later then a reversal operation could be attempted, but the success rate of such an operation is low. If he is in any doubt you should advise him to consider other long-term contraceptive options.

It is important that you explain there is a failure rate of about 1–2 per 1000 for his operation. You should emphasise that he and his partner must continue to use other forms of contraception after his operation until two semen samples have been taken and shown to contain no sperm.

You should explain the risks of the surgery to Mr Walters, including the risks of anaesthesia, bleeding and infection.

Mrs Thomson is a 34-year-old lady under my care. She is 38 weeks pregnant and her fetus has assumed a transverse lie. Attempts to turn him have failed, so I have advised Mrs Thomson that it is in the best interest of herself and her baby for us to deliver him by caesarean section. Unfortunately, Mrs Thomson is profoundly affected by a fear of needles, and for this reason refuses to consent to the operation. I am very concerned for the health of Mrs Thomson and her baby, and feel that her needle phobia is rendering her incompetent to make decisions about her healthcare. Can I proceed anyway without her consent or must I apply to the court?

This is a difficult situation. Although the guidance indicates that if a woman's fear is so overwhelming that she can no longer give a valid consent surgery may proceed in her best interests, it is recommended that you apply to the High Court. This can be done via telephone for expedience and the matter will be resolved with suitable haste.

A case similar to this one was heard in 1997.[5] In that case, the High Court and Court of Appeal both ruled that the woman should have the caesarean section in her best interests, as her needle phobia rendered her mentally incapacitated.

References

1   Butler Sloss LJ in Re MB (Caesarean Section) Times 18th April 1997 Court of Appeal.

2   Beauchamp TL and Childress JF (1994) *Principles of Biomedical Ethics*. Oxford University Press, Oxford.

3 Mason JK, McCall Smith RA and Laurie GT (2002) *Law and Medical Ethics*. Butterworths, London.

4 http://www.hfeae.gov.uk/PressOffice/Backgroundpapers/DonorAnonymity

5 Re MB (an adult: medical treatment) (1997) **2** *FLR*: 426.

CHAPTER 8

The GMC, complaints and whistleblowing

Victoria Tippett and Louise Ma

Doctors and medical students alike work in accordance with the GMC's guidance on the duties of a doctor and make the care of their patients their first concern. They embrace the age-old medical principles of beneficence and non-maleficence, striving to do their patients good but above all to do no harm. Despite such fine intentions both doctors and medical students are human and mistakes happen. It is vital that you know what to do should this occur and that you are aware of the systems in place to protect patients from harm.

This chapter's format differs from that of previous chapters and the text contains several flow diagrams to help explain the systems involved. The topics covered include the role of the GMC, dealing with medical students' health problems and misconduct, dealing with doctors' professional misconduct, dealing with doctors' health problems, whistleblowing and the NHS complaints system.

The General Medical Council (GMC) and its functions

The GMC was established by the Medical Act of 1858 to represent public interest. The British Medical Association already existed, but was mainly acting as a trade union and protecting medical practitioners' interests.

There are 104 members of the GMC in total and within that:

- 54 members are doctors, elected by other doctors on the register
- 25 members are nominated by the Privy Council, which is part of the government. They act as the Final Court of Appeal to the GMC disciplinary rulings and also to some Commonwealth countries
- 25 members are appointed by educational authorities, i.e. medical schools, royal colleges and faculties.

The GMC maintains the official register of medical practitioners which includes all specialties in medicine and surgery. It also gives out advice to patients and doctors and protects the public from doctors who have not been through recognised training. The GMC answers to the Professional Conduct Committee, which is the ultimate tribunal for professional standards. However, any motion for an appeal against a GMC ruling (e.g. with regard to doctors being struck off the medical register) will have to go through the Privy Council.

Dealing with health problems and misconduct of medical students

The GMC has written out a plan to deal with health or conduct problems of medical students as shown below. Although it is not compulsory for all medical schools to comply with this format, it should act as an example to what should be included in individual schools' disciplinary procedures. See Figure 8.1.

The term 'health problem' refers to situations when a medical student's performance and attendance have been severely affected by their mental/physical well-being. Examples include untreated manic depression or acute hepatitis B, but not the occasional cold.

Support for students

Not all universities or NHS trusts have comprehensive services available to help their medical students and staff deal with physical or psychological problems, but most should have at least some of the following support systems available:

- a positive atmosphere in which students/staff feel able to ask for help
- social activities so that students/staff can make new friends and build up a support network for themselves
- a well-organised personal tutor system, so that students/staff know where they can get help
- a counselling service for students/staff to help them deal with traumatic experiences at work or to deal with individuals' mental or physical health issues
- a flexible university listening service that is confidential, e.g. Nightline 020 7631 0101
- a careers counsellor for students who are considering a change of direction
- sessions teaching stress management skills
- sessions teaching clinical staff counselling skills.

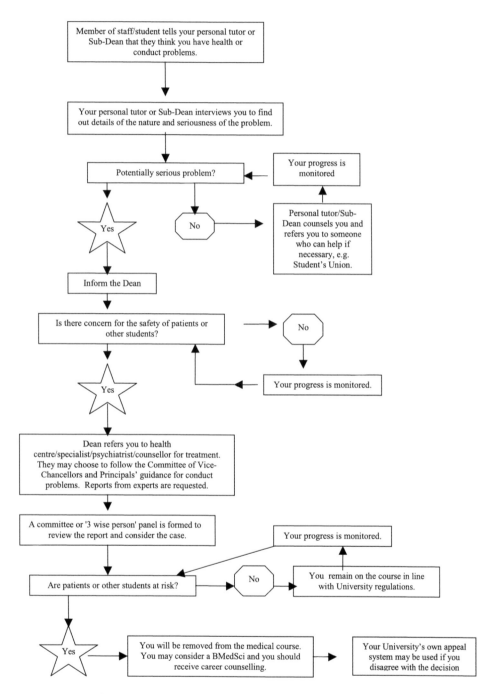

Figure 8.1   Dealing with student health or conduct problems.

Dealing with health problems and misconduct in doctors

The health and misconduct problems of doctors are dealt with on a national level by the GMC, not by an individual hospital or medical school. Although each doctor's case will be different, they go through one of two standard systems, allowing each doctor an opportunity to represent themselves and ensuring their right to a fair hearing.

These processes are simplest in diagrammatic form and are shown in Figures 8.2, 8.3, 8.4 and 8.5.

Both systems have a common appeals process and you have the right to appeal against both Health Committee and Committee on Professional Performance (CPP) decisions (see below and page 90).

Health problems

The Health Committee can receive referrals via one of two routes. The first is from concerned colleagues, pharmacists, employers or patients who suspect that your health is seriously affecting your ability to practise. The second is from another GMC committee which refers a complaint about your performance or conduct to the Health Committee.

The process involved is shown in Figure 8.6.

Figure 8.2 Misconduct (opposite).

    * The screener is nominated by the government from a list of people held by the Department of Health's regional office.

  ** You should now contact your medical defence association. If you are not a member you may wish to contact the BMA or other professional organisation. You may wish to get your own legal advice. Legal Aid is not available and you cannot claim your cost from the other parties involved.

*** The Assessment Review Committee (ARC) comprises 7 members (2 lay) who receive advice from a doctor from your specialty. The decision is NOT whether your performance is seriously deficient, but whether the screener's decision was justified. The meeting is in private – you and the complainant may appear before the ARC. You have the right to a legal representative.

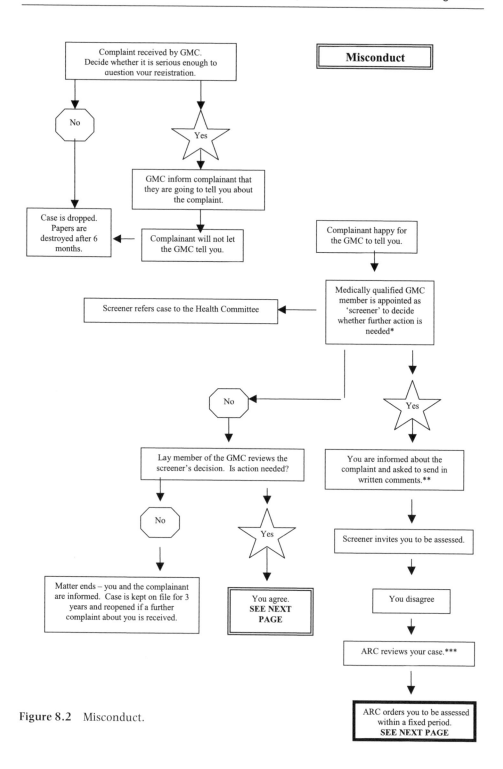

Figure 8.2 Misconduct.

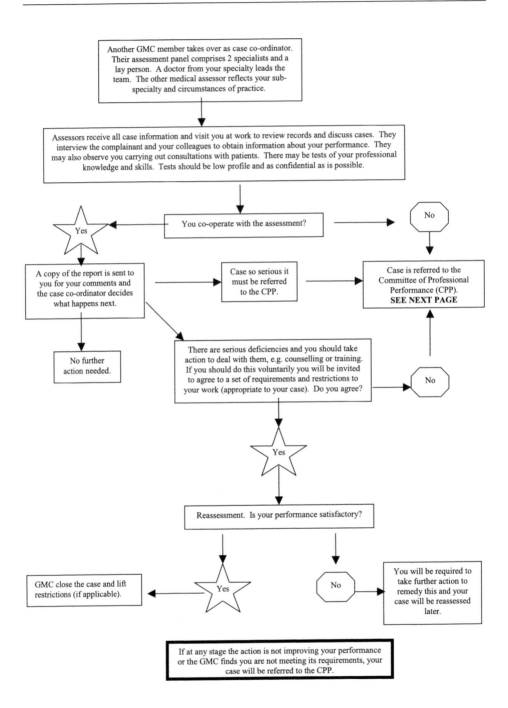

Another GMC member takes over as case co-ordinator. Their assessment panel comprises 2 specialists and a lay person. A doctor from your specialty leads the team. The other medical assessor reflects your sub-specialty and circumstances of practice.

Assessors receive all case information and visit you at work to review records and discuss cases. They interview the complainant and your colleagues to obtain information about your performance. They may also observe you carrying out consultations with patients. There may be tests of your professional knowledge and skills. Tests should be low profile and as confidential as is possible.

You co-operate with the assessment?

Yes

No

A copy of the report is sent to you for your comments and the case co-ordinator decides what happens next.

Case so serious it must be referred to the CPP.

Case is referred to the Committee of Professional Performance (CPP). **SEE NEXT PAGE**

No further action needed.

There are serious deficiencies and you should take action to deal with them, e.g. counselling or training. If you should do this voluntarily you will be invited to agree to a set of requirements and restrictions to your work (appropriate to your case). Do you agree?

No

Yes

Reassessment. Is your performance satisfactory?

GMC close the case and lift restrictions (if applicable).

Yes

No

You will be required to take further action to remedy this and your case will be reassessed later.

If at any stage the action is not improving your performance or the GMC finds you are not meeting its requirements, your case will be referred to the CPP.

Figure 8.3 Assessment ordered by ARC.

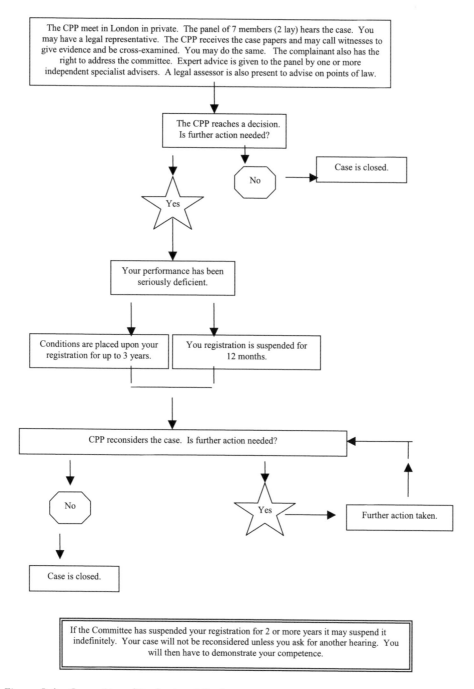

The CPP meet in London in private. The panel of 7 members (2 lay) hears the case. You may have a legal representative. The CPP receives the case papers and may call witnesses to give evidence and be cross-examined. You may do the same. The complainant also has the right to address the committee. Expert advice is given to the panel by one or more independent specialist advisers. A legal assessor is also present to advise on points of law.

The CPP reaches a decision. Is further action needed?

Case is closed.

No

Yes

Your performance has been seriously deficient.

Conditions are placed upon your registration for up to 3 years.

You registration is suspended for 12 months.

CPP reconsiders the case. Is further action needed?

No

Yes

Further action taken.

Case is closed.

If the Committee has suspended your registration for 2 or more years it may suspend it indefinitely. Your case will not be reconsidered unless you ask for another hearing. You will then have to demonstrate your competence.

Figure 8.4   Committee of Professional Performance assessment.

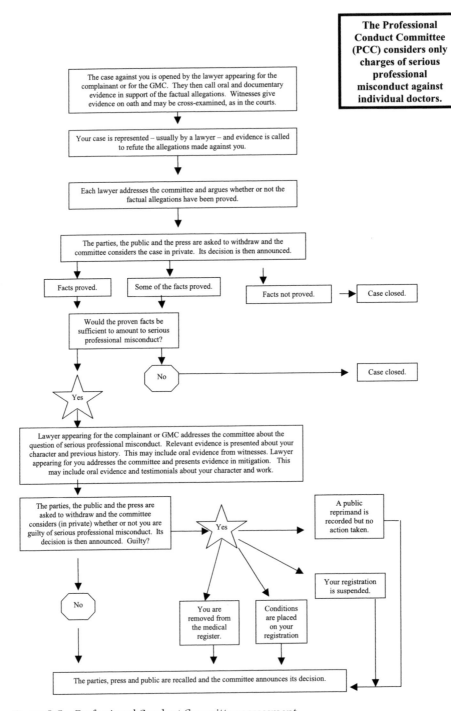

The Professional Conduct Committee (PCC) considers only charges of serious professional misconduct against individual doctors.

The case against you is opened by the lawyer appearing for the complainant or for the GMC. They then call oral and documentary evidence in support of the factual allegations. Witnesses give evidence on oath and may be cross-examined, as in the courts.

Your case is represented – usually by a lawyer – and evidence is called to refute the allegations made against you.

Each lawyer addresses the committee and argues whether or not the factual allegations have been proved.

The parties, the public and the press are asked to withdraw and the committee considers the case in private. Its decision is then announced.

Facts proved.

Some of the facts proved.

Facts not proved. → Case closed.

Would the proven facts be sufficient to amount to serious professional misconduct?

No → Case closed.

Yes

Lawyer appearing for the complainant or GMC addresses the committee about the question of serious professional misconduct. Relevant evidence is presented about your character and previous history. This may include oral evidence from witnesses. Lawyer appearing for you addresses the committee and presents evidence in mitigation. This may include oral evidence and testimonials about your character and work.

The parties, the public and the press are asked to withdraw and the committee considers (in private) whether or not you are guilty of serious professional misconduct. Its decision is then announced. Guilty?

Yes

A public reprimand is recorded but no action taken.

Your registration is suspended.

No

You are removed from the medical register.

Conditions are placed on your registration

The parties, press and public are recalled and the committee announces its decision.

Figure 8.5 Professional Conduct Committee assessment.

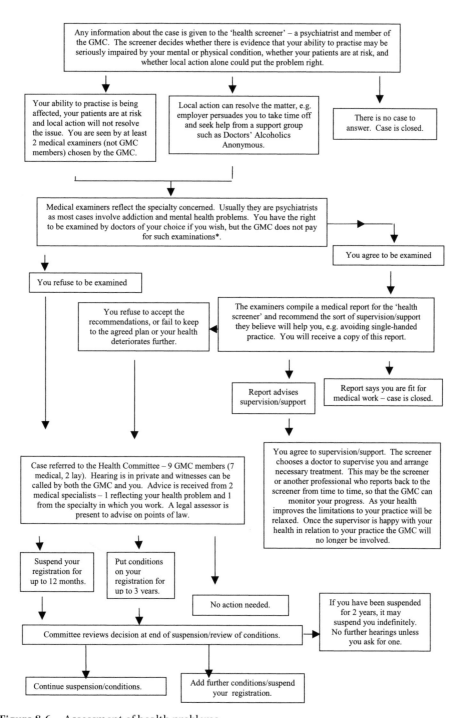

Figure 8.6 Assessment of health problems.

Your right to appeal against both Health Committee and CPP decisions

If the Committee decides to impose conditions or suspend your registration, its decision usually takes effect 28 days after it is announced, and you will be notified of the exact date. However, if the Committee thinks you put others at immediate risk or that it would be in your best interests to stop practising at once it can order immediate suspension of your registration. If you disagree with its decision, you then have the opportunity to apply to the High Court to have that order lifted. You have a period of 28 days to appeal to the Judicial Committee of the Privy Council, but you can only appeal on a point of law – you cannot simply question their judgement. If you have not been suspended immediately, your registration will continue to be valid whilst the appeal is being decided, but if you are appealing against a decision from a resumed hearing following a period of suspension, you will continue to be suspended until the decision is reached.

Revalidation

The GMC has recently publicised plans for revalidation – a process occurring every five years after a doctor has qualified and continuing throughout their working life. From 2005 every doctor will need a licence to practise, which they get via revalidation. The doctor keeps a portfolio of their work and is assessed every five years to ensure they are up to date and fit to practise. If they fail to meet this requirement they can be removed from the GMC's register. For more details see the GMC website: http://www.gmc-uk.org.

Responding appropriately to clinical mistakes

Whenever a doctor or medical student makes a mistake, however small, their personal responsibility is towards the patient. This is why they should explain the wrongdoing to the patient and apologise appropriately. This may be easier said than done if mistakes take a long time to surface and only do so once the patient has already left your care. Furthermore, the repercussions of the mistake might not have put the patient at any risk after all. However, mistakes should always be investigated and rectified in order to safeguard other patients' care in the future. The legal responsibilities involved with clinical mistakes are no different from the personal responsibilities. It is a commonly held misconception that by apologising you are admitting guilt and hence liability under the law. This is **not** the case. A simple apology is not

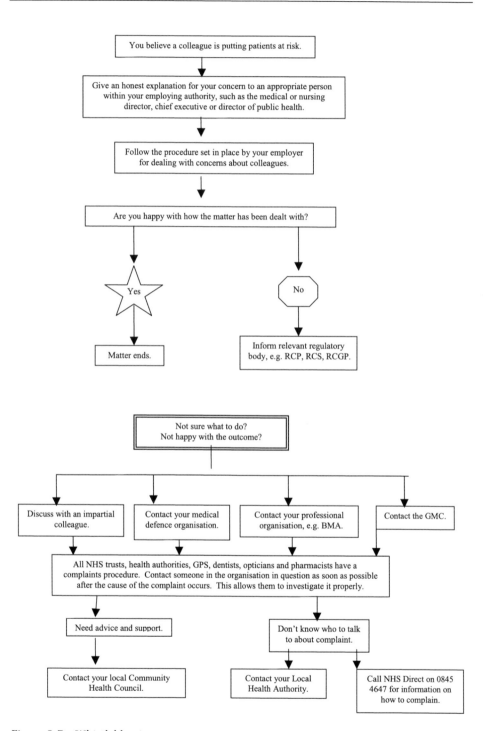

Figure 8.7   Whistleblowing.

only courteous and morally right, but may well dissuade your patient from resorting to official complaints procedures – especially if you are also able to explain why the mistake occurred and what steps have been taken to ensure it will not happen again.

Whistleblowing on unethical and unsafe practices in medicine

Whistleblowing is another word for exposing healthcare professionals who are acting inappropriately within the workplace to the proper authorities, thereby preventing further harm to patients. Under the GMC's guidance on confidentiality: 'disclosure is necessary in the public interest where failure to disclose information may expose patient, or others, to risk of death or serious harm.'[1] Therefore, if such circumstances should arise you should disclose the information to an appropriate person or authority (i.e. if you are a medical student, discuss it with the medical school authorities).

Figure 8.7 shows a step-to-step guide to making a complaint with regards to fellow healthcare professionals. The whistleblower's identity is kept confidential to prevent them from receiving any reprisals. It is hoped that this will encourage more people to come forward with information.

NHS complaints procedure

It is important that you are aware of the NHS complaints procedure and the way in which patients should submit their complaints against NHS staff. Figures 8.8 and 8.9 summarise the process.

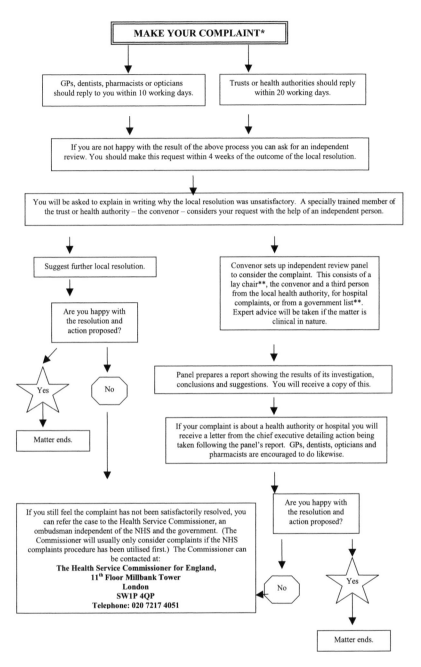

MAKE YOUR COMPLAINT*

GPs, dentists, pharmacists or opticians should reply to you within 10 working days.

Trusts or health authorities should reply within 20 working days.

If you are not happy with the result of the above process you can ask for an independent review. You should make this request within 4 weeks of the outcome of the local resolution.

You will be asked to explain in writing why the local resolution was unsatisfactory. A specially trained member of the trust or health authority – the convenor – considers your request with the help of an independent person.

Suggest further local resolution.

Are you happy with the resolution and action proposed?

Convenor sets up independent review panel to consider the complaint. This consists of a lay chair**, the convenor and a third person from the local health authority, for hospital complaints, or from a government list**. Expert advice will be taken if the matter is clinical in nature.

Yes

No

Matter ends.

Panel prepares a report showing the results of its investigation, conclusions and suggestions. You will receive a copy of this.

If your complaint is about a health authority or hospital you will receive a letter from the chief executive detailing action being taken following the panel's report. GPs, dentists, opticians and pharmacists are encouraged to do likewise.

If you still feel the complaint has not been satisfactorily resolved, you can refer the case to the Health Service Commissioner, an ombudsman independent of the NHS and the government. (The Commissioner will usually only consider complaints if the NHS complaints procedure has been utilised first.) The Commissioner can be contacted at:
The Health Service Commissioner for England,
11ᵗʰ Floor Millbank Tower
London
SW1P 4QP
Telephone: 020 7217 4051

Are you happy with the resolution and action proposed?

No

Yes

Matter ends.

* The complaint needs to include the professional's full name and position and details of what they have done wrong with dates of specific incidents. Copies of any paper or taped evidence that is relevant should be included, along with the names and addresses of any witnesses.

** Nominated by the government from a list of people held by the Department of Health's regional office.

Figure 8.8   The NHS complaints procedure.

Keep up to date

The procedures outlined in this chapter are likely to change over time, particularly with respect to the NHS complaints system. It is vital that you keep

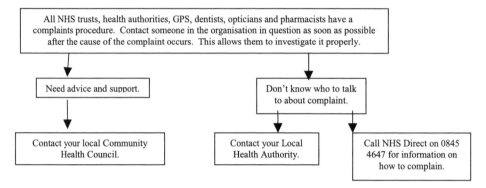

Figure 8.9 The NHS complaints procedure – an overview.

yourself up to date with the latest information both nationally and for the locality in which you study or work. This is most easily achieved over the internet. The most comprehensive websites to use are:

http://www.gmc-uk.org/probdocs/default.htm

This is the page about 'problem doctors' on the GMC's main website (http://www.gmc-uk.org)

http://www.doh.gov.uk/complain.htm

This is the page about the complaints procedures on the Department of Health's website (http://www.doh.gov.uk)

Reference

1 GMC (1995) *Confidentiality – Duties of a Doctor*. General Medical Council, London.

CHAPTER 9

Medical research

Victoria Tippett

Medical research aims to test clinical hypotheses in a scientifically rigorous manner in order to produce objective evidence. As will be explored, the reality of research in the healthcare setting is not black and white. This chapter deals with the legal and ethical issues surrounding medical research, including studies conducted upon children and upon adults who lack the capacity to consent. Stem cell and embryo research are dealt with separately in Chapter 12.

At its best, medical research allows patients both present and future to be offered the most effective and efficacious treatment possible for any given condition. It gives clinicians reliable data upon which to base their everyday clinical decisions. The advocates of medical research are quick to point out that much current treatment is based upon practice trends and its value has never been objectively tested. They maintain that patients are, unwittingly, part of a disorganised trial by clinicians whose results are not being analysed. Those opposed to this view argue that a heavy reliance upon medical research fails to recognise the art involved in the practice of medicine. It regards doctors as machines, with patients being just a disease whose treatment is selected on the basis of research with no attention to individual variation between human beings. Both of these views are extreme and the reality is likely to be somewhere in the middle. It is entirely possible for medical research to inform the decisions doctors make and allow them to select the best available treatment for the individual patient they see before them.

A historical perspective

As recently as the 20th century we have seen appalling abuses of human rights in the name of medical research. In the 1930s and 1940s, the Nazis conducted experiments on Jewish prisoners in concentration camps. These experiments were undertaken without the consent of the participants and involved suffering, pain and often death. More recently, from 1932 to 1972 in Tuskegee,

USA, an ethically questionable experiment was carried out involving 600 black men. Of these men 399 were known to have syphilis (all in the late stages of the disease) and 210 were disease free, acting as controls. This experiment was non-therapeutic. During the period of the study all men received no treatment, despite antibiotics being available for the management of syphilis. Once the details of the Tuskegee study emerged, many wondered why these men agreed to participate. Mostly the subjects were poor and illiterate and those running the study had offered incentives to them to participate. The participants were not told what was being done within the study. At the time this research was being conducted, it was the subject of many reports in leading scientific journals and at conferences, where its moral basis was never questioned.

The Declaration of Helsinki

These tragedies led to the development of several ethical codes for the conduct of research involving human participants. The first was the Nuremberg Code, constructed as a direct result of the war crimes trials after World War Two. Its principles were endorsed by the international medical community in 1964, when the Declaration of Helsinki was drawn up by the World Medical Association. This has been revised several times, most recently in 2002 in the USA. The full text can be found at http://www.wma.net/e/policy/b3.htm, but the following are key excerpts.

> In medical research on human subjects, considerations related to the well-being of the human should take precedence over the interests of science and society.
>
> The primary purpose of medical research involving human subjects is to improve prophylactic, diagnostic and therapeutic procedures and the understanding of the aetiology and pathogenesis of the disease. Even the best proven prophylactic, diagnostic and therapeutic methods must continuously be challenged through research for their effectiveness, efficiency, accessibility and quality.
>
> It is the duty of the physician in medical research to protect the life, health, privacy and dignity of the human subject.
>
> Medical research involving human subjects should be conducted only by scientifically qualified persons and under the supervision of a clinically competent medical person. The responsibility for the human subject must always rest with a medically qualified person and never rest on the subject of the research, even though the subject has given consent.
>
> Physicians should abstain from engaging in research projects involving human subjects unless they are confident that the risks involved have been

adequately assessed and can be satisfactorily managed. Physicians should cease any investigation if the risks are found to outweigh the potential benefits or if there is conclusive proof of positive and beneficial results.

Medical research involving human subjects should only be conducted if the importance of the objective outweighs the inherent risks and burdens to the subject. This is especially important when the human subjects are healthy volunteers.

The subjects must be volunteers and informed participants in the research project.

The physician may combine medical research with medical care only to the extent that the research is justified by its potential prophylactic, diagnostic or therapeutic value. When medical research is combined with medical care, additional standards apply to protect the patients who are research subjects.

The physician should fully inform the patient which aspects of the care are related to the research. The refusal of a patient to participate in a study must never interfere with the patient–physician relationship.

There is also specific guidance, updated in 2002, on the use of placebos:

'. . . [a] placebo-controlled trial may be ethically acceptable, even if proven therapy is available, under the following circumstances:

– Where for compelling and scientifically sound methodological reasons its use is necessary to determine the efficacy or safety of a prophylactic, diagnostic or therapeutic method; or
– Where a prophylactic, diagnostic or therapeutic method is being investigated for a minor condition and the patients who receive placebo will not be subject to any additional risk of serious or irreversible harm.'

The law

The Declaration of Helsinki underpins the ethical and legal framework within which medical research is conducted throughout the world. In England and Wales the law relating to medical research is not easy to access and is often piecemeal. If a person voluntarily participating in a study is injured, they can make a claim for compensation under the law of tort (the law that also applies to medical negligence claims). This rests upon the duty of care owed to the participant by the study's organiser. Case law to act as guidance in this area is sadly lacking.

In relation to patients or participants incompetent to consent, the law in Scotland is very specific. There, the Adults with Incapacity (Scotland) Act 2000 s51 regulates such research (*see* Appendix). In England and Wales there is no such statute, although the Law Commission in England in 1995 recommended legislation to authorise non-therapeutic research on incompetent adults. The issues surrounding medical research involving incompetent adults are discussed more fully on pages 100–1.

GMC guidance

The General Medical Council (GMC) has issued very clear and comprehensive guidance on the role and responsibilities of doctors in relation to research. This can be found in full at their website http://www.gmc-uk.org/standards/research.htm or in their booklet: 'Research: the role and responsibilities of doctors'. It emphasises that you must be satisfied that when undertaking therapeutic research the potential benefits to the patients outweigh the foreseeable risks. It also reinforces the need for ethical approval from a research ethics committee.

You should also ensure that your participants, be they patients or volunteers, understand they are participating in research and the results are not predictable. Participants' consent should be obtained and recorded unless an ethics committee has given specific approval to *not* obtain consent. A participant's right to confidentiality must always be respected. For studies involving records rather than patients themselves, the principles of research on humans still apply. It is essential that you have the authority to access the data you propose to use.

The GMC's website and booklet give detailed advice on putting these principles into practice and should be a first port of call when you are designing your research project.

Many of the royal colleges also issue their own specific guidance. That of the Royal College of Physicians is particularly good, and is published as '*Royal College of Physicians Guidelines on the Practice of Ethical Committees in Medical Research involving Human Subjects*' (3rd edition, August 1997) publications @rcplondon.ac.uk

Key ethical issues within medical research

Quality of the research

In order to justify any risk or inconvenience to patients, no matter how small, the research must be of a good quality, so that the results it yields are useful. Poor-quality research can put current patients at unnecessary risk and put future patients at risk of harm.

Informed consent

Patients must be adequately informed about why the trial is being done, what it will achieve and what will be involved for them personally. They should also be able to withdraw from the trial at any point in time without this having a detrimental effect on their overall treatment.

Ability to consent to harm and accept risks

Opinions differ on how much harm a patient should be able to consent to. Many argue that just as some people choose to participate in dangerous sports, so they should be able to choose to participate in research that involves some risk to themselves, as long as their consent to take part is informed and freely given. However, the guidance of the GMC and Royal College of Physicians recommends that the patient should be at no more than minimal harm (likened to that of making a normal car journey).

Doctor–patient relationship

It is important that participation in medical research does not harm the doctor–patient relationship. A patient must not feel under pressure to take part in a study to please their doctor or to accept treatment that they are not happy with because their doctor can only give treatment in accordance with the protocol of the study. For this reason patients are often recruited to research projects by people other than their usual doctor and the decision as to which treatment they are offered is made by a computer or researcher who is independent of the doctor–patient encounter.

Confidentiality

Patient confidentiality should be respected at all times. Patient notes may not routinely be used for research purposes and the consent of the patient concerned should be gained before researchers are allowed to access patient records. The GMC guidelines state that:

'Where it is not practicable for the person who holds the records either to obtain express consent to disclosure, or to anonymise records, data may be disclosed for research, provided participants have been given information about access to their records, and about their right to object. Any objection must be respected. Usually such disclosures will be made to allow a person outside the research team to anonymise the records or to identify participants who may be invited to participate in a study.

Such disclosures must be kept to the minimum necessary for the purpose. In all such cases you must be satisfied that participants have been told or have had access to written material informing them:

- that their records may be disclosed to persons outside the team which provided their care
- of the purpose and extent of the disclosure, for example, to produce anonymised data for use in research, epidemiology or surveillance
- that the person given access to records will be subject to a duty of confidentiality
- that they have a right to object to such a process and that their objection will be respected, except where the disclosure is essential to protect the patient, or someone else, from risk of death or serious harm.'

Payment

Many argue that participants should be able to receive payment for their involvement in research, but the Department of Health (DoH) guidelines state that volunteers should only receive payment in cash or kind for expense, time and inconvenience incurred. The DoH is concerned that payment should not induce people to take part in studies against their better judgement.

Those who cannot consent

Those who cannot consent were once used for research without due regard to their wishes and needs. This was followed by a dramatic shift to paternalistic protection of the rights of those who cannot consent, which unfortunately resulted in valuable research (which could have benefited many patients) not being conducted. As described previously, legal guidance in this area in England and Wales is sadly lacking, but the GMC guidance gives a framework within which to conduct such studies.

'Research into conditions that are not linked to incapacity should never be undertaken with adults with incapacity if it could equally well be done with other adults. It should be limited to areas of research related to the participants' incapacity or to physical illnesses that are linked to their incapacity. If you involve this group of people in research you must demonstrate that:

- it could be of direct benefit to their health; or
- it is of special benefit to the health of people in the same age group with the same state of health; or
- that it will significantly improve the scientific understanding of the adult's incapacity leading to a direct benefit to them or to others with the same incapacity; and
- the research is ethical and will not cause the participants emotional, physical or psychological harm; and
- the person does not express objections physically or verbally.

You must also ensure that participants' right to withdraw from the research is respected at all times. Any sign of distress, pain or indication of refusal irrespective of whether or not it is given in a verbal form should be considered as implied refusal.'

Children

Research involving children is a highly emotive area. The GMC issues specific guidance which acknowledges that children and young people are vulnerable members of society. It is important to protect their '. . . ethical, physical, mental and emotional rights and ensure that they are not exploited'. It also stresses that, as when treating children, if they are not competent to consent themselves ('Gillick competent') then you must obtain the consent of someone with parental responsibility for that child.

The Child Health: Ethics Advisory Committee of the Royal College of Paediatricians has drawn up specific guidelines for the ethical conduct of medical research involving children. They can be found at:

http://adc.bmjjournals.com/cgi/content/full/archdischild%3b82/2/177? maxtoshow=%3feaf

Other groups involved in research

Students and prisoners

The role of volunteer participants, medical students and prisoners are all areas of special interest in their own right. Medical students may come under pressure to take part in studies in order to please their tutors or lecturers, thus rendering their consent to participate invalid as it is not freely given. In some circumstances students may also be under financial pressure to participate in studies for which they would not normally be prepared to volunteer. Prisoners are also a special group. They are often considered an easily accessible study population, but prisoners may participate in studies in order to gain better treatment whilst in prison, or to avoid punishment. This chapter does not have the space for a thorough exploration of these issues and I would direct you to a text such as *The Ethics of Medical Research on Humans* by Claire Foster[1] or *Law and Medical Ethics* by Mason, McCall Smith and Laurie[2] for further information.

Animals

The use of animals for medical research is also an area of constant debate. Is it right to experiment upon animals at all? Do animals have rights of their own as creatures able to feel pain? Or is animal research justified so long as it prevents human suffering? Much work has been done in this area of ethics. Good introductory texts and articles include Frey and Paton,[3] Midgley,[4] Regan and Singer,[5] and Regan.[6]

Organs and tissues

There has been much interest in the retention of patients' organs for use in clinical research since the Alder Hey enquiry in 2001. The Retained Organs Commission, chaired by Professor Margot Brazier, can issue specific guidance to institutions or individuals wishing to use patients' organs or tissues for clinical research. The principles of research upon human subjects, particularly that of informed consent, apply equally to tissue-based research. More information can be found at http://www.nhs.uk/retainedorgans/

Following the above enquiries, the government drafted the Human Tissue Bill, which is likely to become law in the near future at the time of writing. The Bill repeals the Human Tissue Act 1961 and the Human Tissue Act (Northern Ireland) 1962, the Anatomy Act 1984 and the Human Organ Transplants Act 1989. There will therefore be one Act to cover the use of human bodies and their component parts during both life and death.

The Bill covers human material – all parts of the human body excluding gametes, hair and nails and embryos when outside of their mother's body. Removal of surgical tissue from living patients is still governed by the patient's consent to treatment.

The key elements of the Bill are that in order to legally remove, retain or use body parts you must obtain the person's consent during their life, or the consent of someone the person nominated to represent him/her after death, or the consent of the person's 'nearest relative' or another person close to them during their life. In addition to this, the government proposes establishing the Human Tissue Authority to regulate tissue use and ensure that the requirements of the Bill are met.

In June 2004, Parliament issued amendments to the Bill, principally that material from living human patients may be used for research and education without specific consent from the donor. Further details of these amendments can be found at http://www.publications.parliament.uk/pa/ cm200304/cmbills/049/2004049.htm and http://www.mrc.ac.uk/pdf-htb_ views_updated_25jun04.pdf

Post mortems

Hospital post mortems (PMs) are carried out to allow clinicians to identify the pathological processes occurring in a patient at the time of their death. Unlike a coroner's PM, where the pathologist looks simply for the cause of death and no further, a hospital PM can examine many systems and reveal much more information about a patient's illness. Hospital PMs are usually undertaken where there has been some uncertainty about the patient's illness or where it has unique or fascinating features. They are designed to inform and educate the clinician or clinical team requesting the PM, to improve their future work. In some centres they are referred to as a PM for clinical research. If you and your team would like to conduct such a PM you should raise this as soon as possible after death with the relatives of the deceased. In order to undertake a hospital PM, the relatives must give their informed consent and there is a lengthy document to be filled out by yourself and the relatives. It is a difficult time at which to discuss such issues and many families do not like to think of pathologists cutting their relatives open. It is therefore unsurprising that in modern times few hospital PMs are carried out. If you and your team wish to request a hospital PM, discuss it with the patient's relatives and contact your local Patient's Office who will be able to give you advice and supply you with the relevant consent forms.

Stopping a trial early

The GMC guidance states that if your trial is showing clear evidence of benefit or, conversely, harm, it is unethical to continue the trial as if uncertainty persisted. When planning your trial it is important to include interim analyses at various points in time. These analysis points allow you to review the data collected so far without this wreaking havoc with the statistical analysis of your trial at its endpoint. If, when you conduct your interim analysis, the data show clear benefit or harm you are morally obliged to stop the trial and publish the data you have collected so far, with recommendations based on your findings.

For example, in 1998 a large breast cancer trial was stopped early as its results showed that tamoxifen halved the rate of recurrence of breast cancer.[7] Critics argued that long-term follow-up data on risks of treatments such as tamoxifen are at risk of being lost if trials are stopped as soon as data for efficacy have been found.

EU Clinical Trials Directive

The EU Clinical Trials Directive was first written in April 2001 by the European Parliament and the Council of the European Union. The directive was fully implemented on 1 May 2004.

Article 3 describes the protection of clinical trial subjects. It advises that the risks and benefits are weighed up for the participant and present or future patients, and that the participant has the opportunity to question the investigating team about the project. It also states that ethics committee approval is always necessary. The participant has the right to withdraw their consent at any time.

Projects should have indemnity (insurance) to cover the liability of the investigating team and a doctor or dentist, as is appropriate, should oversee any medical care or treatment involved in the research.

Article 4 relates specifically to trials involving minors. It stipulates that the child's parents must give their informed consent *and* that that consent must represent the child's will. As in Article 3, this consent may be withdrawn at any time. No incentives should be given, but compensation may sometimes be appropriate. Research involving children should relate to a condition which the child has himself/herself or be of a nature that it can only be undertaken upon minors. The project must have ethics committee approval and the interests of the child must always prevail over those of science and society.

Article 5 relates to trials involving adults unable to give their consent. In addition to the requirements of Article 3, the informed consent of the legal representative of the adult must have been obtained and this should represent the will of the adult (or presumed will of the adult). It may be withdrawn at any time. The adult should have received information about the risks and benefits of the trial suitable to their level of understanding.

Research involving adults unable to consent should relate to a life-threatening or debilitating condition from which they suffer. The directive specifically states that in these cases there should be grounds for expecting that the administering of the medicinal product being tested will produce a benefit to the adult patient, outweighing the risks or producing no risk at all.

Article 6 describes how ethics committees should operate. They are advised to consider the protocol, brochure of the investigator, suitability of the investigator and their team, quality of the facilities and adequacy of the information given to participants.

For more details see:

- http://mrc.ac.uk/index/current-research/current-clinical_research/ funding-clinical_research_governance/current-eu_clinical_trials_ directive.htm or

- http://medicines.mhra.gov.uk/ourwork/licensingmeds/types/clintrialdir.htm#impuk

Ethics committees

It is recommended that all research proposals gain ethical approval before they are commenced. Most funding bodies will require researchers to have gained research ethics committee approval before they will consider the application. The process is, however, daunting to the newcomer. Over the following pages, the structure and terminology of research ethics committees will be explained, using flow diagrams to take you through the application process step by step.

The Central Office for Research Ethics Committees (COREC) works on behalf of the Department of Health in England and co-ordinates the local and multi-centre research ethics committees across the country. These research ethics committees (RECs) consist of clinicians, researchers and lay people and give independent advice to researchers, participants in studies, funders, sponsors and employers on the extent to which research proposals comply with recognised ethical research standards. Their aim is to protect the rights and well-being of research participants.

Which research proposals need to go to an REC?

All those involving NHS patients, their relatives, NHS staff or tissue/organs/bodies of NHS patients. (For more specific guidance see http://www.corec.org.uk/) Occasionally RECs will offer advice to private sector companies, charities, the Medical Research Council or universities about their research projects.

Which REC do I apply to?

As principal researcher, you should apply to the local research ethics committee (LREC) for the locality in which you are based. If your local LREC does not have the capacity to handle your application within a reasonable time, you can apply to another LREC within the area covered by your local strategic health authority.

Do I have to apply to anyone else?

When you have a favourable ethical opinion from one LREC, you have to apply to the other relevant LRECs within the same strategic health authority for locality assessment. You should report the approval of locality issue to your lead LREC (the one granting ethical approval). Permission should also be gained from the host NHS trust or other NHS organization before you begin your research.

What if my research is spread over an area greater than just my local strategic health authority?

Multicentre research is defined as 'research taking place within the boundaries of two or more research "sites" '. So, for example, if you work in the North East London Strategic Health Authority, but you are collaborating with a colleague working in the South West London Strategic Health Authority, your research is called multicentre. If your research covers 2–4 sites, you can apply to one LREC in each area or to the Multicentre Research Ethics Committee (MREC). If your research covers five or more sites you must apply to the MREC. Once you have ethical approval from the MREC you then need to apply to all the relevant LRECs, but just for locality assessment.

How do I apply?

The applications forms and addresses of LRECs and the MREC can be found at: http://www.corec.org.uk/
    The flowcharts in Figures 9.1 and 9.2 summarise the process graphically.

 Where you stand

- Plan your study carefully, as far in advance as possible.
- Ensure that all participants are placed at minimal harm when undertaking your study.
- Plan in interim analyses from the outset, so you can stop the study early if necessary.
- Apply for ethical approval in good time before you propose to begin your research study.
- Obtain informed consent, preferably in writing, from all your participants.

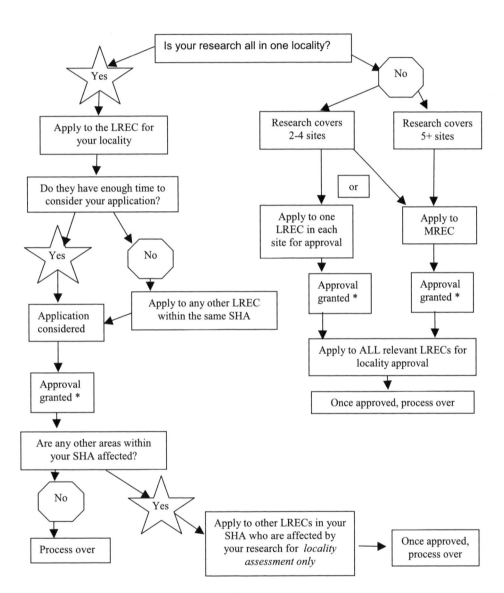

Figure 9.1 Applying to a local research ethics committee.

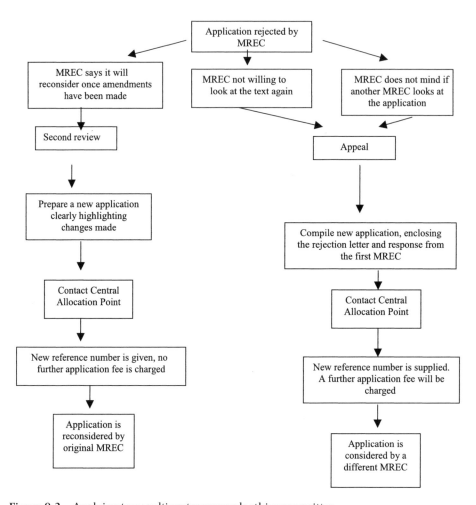

Figure 9.2 Applying to a multicentre research ethics committee.

Where you fall

- If you harm any participants during your study, you will be liable under the law of tort. You will have breached your duty of care to that person and may be liable to pay them damages if a court finds you to have been negligent.
- If you cause physical harm to a person then you may be personally guilty of assault under criminal law. This involves the risk of imprisonment.
- If you fail to gain ethical approval for your research you are unlikely to receive funding for the research and almost all major medical journals will refuse to publish your data, rendering your efforts futile.

Cases

I want to do a study looking at the blood pressure of patients aged over 50 in my GP practice. What do I need to do in order to get ethics committee approval for my study?

It is important to start planning your study as soon as possible. Decide on your hypothesis or aims and construct a methodology. You must draw up information for the participants which enables them to give their informed consent to participate in the study and lets them know that they are free to withdraw at any time without this jeopardising the treatment they receive from you. In a community setting such as yours it is particularly important to ensure that the study does not jeopardise your relationship with your patients. In your plan, identify any potential ethical issues that may arise and outline how you will address these. Then look at the website http://www.corec.org.uk/ to obtain the application form relevant to your LREC. Your LREC will usually hold monthly meetings, and your application should be sent for consideration at the next meeting.

I am conducting a research study and my data so far show the new treatment for hypertension is far better than the existing gold standard treatment I was comparing it to, but I am only halfway through my study. What do I do now?

Morally there are two arguments to consider. The first is that, given your data so far show clear benefit of the new treatment over the old one, it is wrong to keep giving your patients the old treatment when you are sure that you have another, better option. The second is that if you stop your study early, you may fail to discover long-term risks associated with your new treatment. Generally the consensus tends to fall in favour of the former position, but you should discuss this with your research colleagues.

The relevant legal issues involve tort and a claim in negligence. For a claim in negligence to succeed you must have a duty of care to the person, you must be shown to have breached that duty and as a result of the breach, the person must have suffered harm. Therefore, in theory at least, if you continue the study and half of the subjects are being given a poorer treatment, it could be argued that you are breaching your duty of care to them. If, as a result of their blood pressure being less well controlled, they suffer a stroke, it could be argued that you had caused that harm by your negligent actions in not stopping the study. It should be noted that there is no case law in this specific area and it would be exceedingly difficult for a patient to prove that your actions had led to their subsequent stroke, but it is an issue that you should consider.

If you have concerns about how stopping the trial early might affect your data, talk to your statistician.

References

1 Foster C (2001) *The Ethics of Medical Research on Humans.* Cambridge University Press, Cambridge.

2 Mason JK, McCall Smith RA and Laurie GT (2002) *Law and Medical Ethics.* Butterworths, London.

3 Frey RG and Paton W (1983) Vivisection, morals and medicine: an exchange. *Journal of Medical Ethics.* **9**: 94–7 and 102–4.

4 Midgley M (1983) *Animals and Why They Matter.* Penguin, Harmondsworth, Middlesex.

5 Regan T and Singer P (1989) *Animal Rights and Human Obligations.* Lawrence Erlbaum, Englewood Cliffs, New Jersey.

6 Regan T (1983) *The Case for Animal Rights.* Berkley, New York.

7 Josefson D (1998) News: Breast cancer trial stopped early. *BMJ.* **316**: 1185.

CHAPTER 10

Rationing and resources

Victoria Tippett

The National Health Service (NHS) was created on 5 July 1948 by Aneurin Bevan[1] of the Labour Party. The aim of the NHS has always been to deliver healthcare free to all at the point of need, but need can prove difficult to define, as will be explored in this chapter. Bevan foresaw:

> 'We shall never have all we need . . . Expectations will always exceed capacity. The service must always be changing, growing and improving – it must always appear inadequate.'[2]

Resources will always be finite and the claims made upon them infinite. This begs several questions.

What should the NHS fund?

In an age where new technologies and designer drugs continue to take medicine forwards, but at a cost, what should the NHS pay for? The latest treatments are also the most expensive and so overall NHS costs tend to increase as the best available treatment is usually also the most costly.

Who should the NHS fund?

The demographics of each area of the country are different and these different populations will make different demands upon the health budget. How do we compare competing claims on a regional scale? Should we fund treatments for everyone on a national basis or can 'postcode prescribing' be justified?

The background to resource allocation is essentially political. Governments set the health budget and weigh the demands of the NHS against those of defence or social services. With each successive government eager to make its mark on the NHS and win the votes of the general public, how can the health service achieve any stability in its management? What influence does this constantly shifting political landscape have on the resources of the NHS and their allocation? This chapter will explore how resources can be fairly distributed and their effects maximised for the benefit of all patients.

The law

Before the NHS was created in 1948, there existed two classes of doctors. A few were fashionable and only dealt with wealthy citizens. The rest worked with panel patients. These patients paid the doctor a small amount of money each week to ensure they could have treatment when they were sick. People could not always afford panel payments and self-help books were widely used. The local pharmacist would also be on hand to advise on medicine for simple common problems.[3]

This system changed completely in 1948 when the NHS was created. Along with the organizational change came a certain amount of statute, including the NHS Act 1977. This act gives the Secretary of State a statutory duty to provide hospital accommodation. There have been several cases where patients have attempted to bring an action against the Secretary of State for failing to provide for their particular health needs. The courts have been very reluctant to interfere with how resources are allocated. It has been stated by an appeal judge that for the Secretary of State to fail in the above duty, he or she must be acting thoroughly unreasonably. No court has yet found the Secretary of State guilty of this.

Whilst the Secretary of State controls overall funding, from 1980 health authorities have been required to balance their own individual budgets. Since this time cases *have* been brought by patients against them, but the courts have stated that they '. . . cannot arrange the lists in the hospital . . . and should not be asked to intervene'.[4] Primary care trusts (PCTs) were first established in April 2000 and have control of local health budgets. As yet no case law is available involving PCTs.

A right to resources?

The Human Rights Act, incorporated into UK law in 1998, is likely to have a major impact upon resource allocation and cases involving patients' claims of unfair allocation. As yet this area has not been fully explored in the courts. The implications of the Human Rights Act 1998 and the European Convention on Human Rights are more fully discussed in Chapter 11.

It is, however, possible to discuss the concept of a right to healthcare and how one can attempt to balance the rights of individuals against the rights of the community when allocating resources.

The World Health Organization (WHO) states that 'Health is a state of complete physical, mental and social well-being and not merely the absence of disease or infirmity'.[5] Given such a broad definition, if the NHS were to meet all the nation's health needs the demands on its funds would be limitless. For example, the contentious areas of cosmetic surgery and gender reassignment surgery would be funded by the NHS if it sought to meet the strict demands laid out by the WHO. At present the NHS does not offer these services to all patients.

When viewed as a whole the problems of health resource allocation seem impossible to resolve. How are we to choose between paying for cancer treatment or diabetic medications? Ethicists have approached the problem from several different angles over the years. The key approaches use principles of beneficence or justice.

Beneficence

Beneficence describes actions that contribute to a person's well-being and so *benefit* them. More than just non-maleficence (not doing harm), beneficence demands that positive actions are undertaken to benefit others. Within beneficence is described the principle of utility. This requires the moral agent (you) to balance the benefits and the drawbacks of a course of action to produce the best overall results. When analysing treatments, the terms cost-effectiveness or cost–benefit are often used. Although cost usually refers to the financial burden incurred, it can also mean cost to a patient in terms of pain, suffering or shortened life span. Benefit may simply refer to a reduction in risk, but can also represent a positive outcome such as a life saved or improvement in quality of life. How much we value a particular cost or benefit then determines how we balance our cost–benefit calculations and reach our decisions. Cost–benefit analyses deal in financial terms and values, whereas cost-effectiveness analyses measure benefits in other ways such as by improved quality of life.

Justice

Principles of justice allow us to search for a fair and equitable way of dividing limited resources between a population. Theories of justice can be further subdivided into:

- utilitarian: where it is the job of justice to maximise the value (or good) derived from a given situation

- libertarian: where the free market is allowed to operate and distribution occurs on the basis of ability to pay
- communitarian: where the community has a responsibility to the individual and vice versa
- egalitarian: where all persons should receive an equal distribution of goods, including healthcare, or an equal opportunity of access to resources.

Famous ethicists who write about healthcare rationing include John Rawls[6] and Norman Daniels.[7,8] Rawls described the 'veil of ignorance' for just distribution of any resource. Here, the distribution of the resource in question is decided by persons under a veil of ignorance – unaware what their position in society is. It rests on the assumption that those who have no knowledge of what their position in the community is will come up with a system that is fair and reasonable for whichever part they later have to play in that community.

Daniels argues for a system of healthcare based upon fair opportunity. No person should receive social benefits on the basis of an advantage that they have but do not deserve. Equally, they should not be denied social benefits on the basis of a disadvantage they have but did not deserve.

The meeting of basic needs?

Although controversy persists as to what constitutes a basic or fundamental need, most ethicists are agreed that there should be provision of health and social care so that every individual has their basic needs met. These basic needs include food, clothing, shelter and health. Broader lists include education, employment opportunity and privacy. When defining basic needs it can be argued that a need is something that is essential to autonomous functioning and that it does not rely upon a person being aware of its existence. In other words you do not need to *know* that you need shelter to need it. This is in contrast to wants or desires, which are psychological and require the individual to be aware of the perceived need. You have to *know* that you want something in order to want it.

It could therefore be argued that all persons require that their basic needs be met and so healthcare should be available to all persons. Unfortunately these theories do not tell us how to discriminate between the *competing* needs of individuals.

Rationing frameworks – QALYs and SAVEs

Quality-adjusted life-years (QALYs) were devised as a way of comparing the cost-effectiveness of different treatments, taking into account not just life-years saved, but also the quality of those years. QALYs provide numerical values as follows:

1 year healthy life expectancy $= 1$
1 year unhealthy life expectancy $= <1$
(*the more unhealthy, the lower the value*)
Death $= 0$
A life considered worse than death <0
(*a minus score*).

(Not all ethicists agree that it is possible for a life to be worse than death and some consider any form of life to be better than if that person were dead.)

Whilst seeming to give a neat numerical value to aid the making of difficult decisions, QALYs have several faults. Their judgements about the value of the patient's life are always made in that patient's best interests, but are made by a third party. How can someone else fairly assess the value a person places on their own life at any given time? Are QALYs therefore only safe to use when comparing one treatment option for a patient against another treatment for the same patient? John Harris has argued strongly against QALYs.[9] He maintains that they detract from the fact that life is intrinsically valuable and that we should be saving lives, not life-years. He argues that the important fact is the value a person places upon his or her own life at a given time and thus a patient in the last stages of metastatic breast cancer with two weeks to live may value their life just as much as the patient with chronic renal failure who may live for five years with the aid of dialysis.

Although QALYs are widely discussed in medical literature, there are alternative systems that have been proposed. One such system is saved young life equivalents (SAVEs). In this system maximum benefit is defined as saving the life of a young person and restoring them to full health. The outcomes of all other treatments are then assigned a comparative value relative to the saving of the young person's life. This system is inherently ageist, but does it successfully translate into practice a feeling often voiced in society that the young have a stronger entitlement to healthcare so that they may live to experience life, whereas the old have already enjoyed many years and should, if necessary, make way for the young?

Is random allocation the answer?

Given the difficulties encountered when attempting to implement any of the above schemes, you would be forgiven for thinking that random allocation may provide the answer to equitable resource distribution. However, whilst it can be argued that such a system would be very just, it would ignore patient welfare. It would remove clinical judgement from the equation and render patients more like numbers in a giant lottery than unique human beings. Random allocation may be easy, but it is not the answer.

What system does the UK use at the moment?

The NHS is funded by taxpayers. The proportion of tax spent on the NHS, as opposed to defence or education, is decided by the government. As the amount of tax a person pays is related to their income, the principle is that those who can afford to contribute more to the system than the less well off.

The NHS Plan details the government's strategy for investment and reform. It includes the devolution of power from the government and Department of Health to local health authorities and frontline staff, the setting of national targets and monitoring of performance by an independent body, the Commission for Health Improvement (CHI). Under the new Health and Social Care Act 2003, a new body – the Commission for Health Audit and Inspection (CHAI)[10] – will replace CHI, the National Care Standards Commission and the Audit Commission from 1 April 2004. The Health and Social Care Act 2003 not only establishes the CHAI but also establishes NHS foundation trusts. Those trusts performing best nationally will be considered for foundation status. Such foundation trusts will not be subject to direction by the Secretary of State, but will have their performance monitored by an independent regulator. Whilst still being a part of the NHS, the trust will have greater financial and management freedoms.[11]

The National Institute for Clinical Excellence (NICE) was set up to evaluate new therapies and ensure that the availability of treatments did not depend on which area of the country you are in. The NHS Modernisation Agency was created to spread best practice across different areas of the organization. Further details of the NHS Plan can be found at http://www.nhs.uk/nationalplan/

What systems do other countries use?

In the USA, Medicare and Medicaid provide healthcare for those who cannot afford private cover. Medicare is a prepaid medical insurance plan for all members of society through the social security system. Medicaid applies specifically to low-income persons and is part of the USA's federal state welfare structure.[12]

In France and Germany there is a social insurance system in which individuals make payments. Most of the costs of these systems fall to the employer and the employee, so fewer people contribute than in a tax-based system such as that in the UK. Therefore a smaller proportion of the total population support the nation's healthcare.

Are these systems better than ours?

Opinion is divided. The government, unsurprisingly, thinks not. It argues that in countries such as Germany and France there may be more resources available to health, but they are spent inefficiently. In the USA there is a huge gulf between the level of service received by those using Medicaid or Medicare and those with private health insurance, with those using the former receiving a lower standard of care. No system is perfect and the debate continues.

Responsibility and rationing

No chapter on rationing and resource allocation would be complete without mention of the minefield that is individual responsibility for health. To what extent should individuals be held responsible for their own illnesses? Are smokers responsible for their subsequent coronary artery disease or lung cancer? Are snowboarders responsible for their broken legs? The debate rages. In some cases, cause and effect are easier to tie together. Some forms of lung cancer occur almost exclusively in smokers. If the snowboarder had not chosen that particular course they would not have fallen and broken their leg. However, in both examples other factors of which the patient is unaware play a role. The smoker may have a genetic predisposition to the development of cancerous change in their cells. The smoking has simply increased the chance of them developing the cancer. The smoker knew he was increasing his risk of getting lung cancer, but could not know that it would definitely happen to him. The snowboarding episode is an accident. The snowboarder may have hit a rock that she had not seen under the snow and hence fallen and broken her leg. Whilst she was aware there was a danger of her breaking a bone if she went snowboarding, she could not be sure that it would definitely happen to her.

There is no right or wrong answer, but if we do hold both individuals as responsible for their resulting health problems, to what extent are they culpable? And if culpable, should they be made to contribute financially to the cost of their treatment? Can healthcare professionals morally refuse to treat patients without payment where they are wholly or partially responsible for their illnesses? Or should we be taxing activities that endanger people's health like smoking, sports or driving cars and using that tax to directly benefit the health service?

There are no right and wrong answers in this area, but as healthcare professionals we are responsible for resource allocation on a small scale, every day. With this comes the responsibility to consider the moral basis of our decisions and the broader context in which we take them.

 # Where you stand

- Health resources are finite.

- Competing claims for health resources must be judged fairly on the basis of need.
- Primary care trusts control local health budgets and allocate resources.
- The NHS Plan details the bigger picture of the spending plans for the NHS.

 # Where you fall

- If you discriminate unfairly when allocating health resources you may be liable under the Disability Discrimination Act 1995.
- A trust or government may not impose blanket bans on treatments unless they can be shown to be of no medical benefit.

Cases

> I work in a busy transplant unit in London. My consultant has decided to refuse to offer a liver transplant to anyone who has alcoholic liver disease because she feels that their disease is their own fault and that they will ruin the donor liver by continued drinking. She does not think any drunk can truly give up alcohol and they will all relapse in the end. I disagree with her but feel powerless as she is my boss. What can I do?

To justify her argument your consultant would have to show that there was no benefit to a person who drinks excessive quantities of alcohol in replacing their failing liver, on the basis that they would destroy the donor liver too. This would be difficult, as the recipient would initially experience the benefit of the donor liver, even if in the longer term they damaged that organ by their continued drinking. It sounds as if she is making a moral judgement on the lifestyle choices made by these patients and is using this judgement to form clinical choices, which is not justified.

You are in a difficult position and it will not be easy to discuss this with your consultant. You should explain to your consultant what your objections are and attempt to persuade her to change her policy so that each patient is assessed as an individual.

The government and the law do not support blanket rulings as to the allocation of resources. In the case of *R v Secretary of State for Health, ex p Pfizer Ltd* [1999] Lloyd's Rep Med 289, (2000) 51 BMLR 189, the High Court declared the government's blanket ban on the provision of sildenafil (Viagra) at NHS expense interfered with doctors' professional judgements.

I work as a specialist registrar in Plastic Surgery. I saw a patient the other day in the outpatient clinic who wanted breast enlargement surgery. She told me that she was undergoing great psychological suffering as a result of her small breasts and needed the operation to restore her mental health. When I explained that our NHS trust will not fund such operations, she became very angry, and told me that I was denying her her human rights. She shouted that she has a right to treatment. Is she correct?

No, she is not correct. No court has established a right to treatment for patients and judges have deliberately avoided becoming involved in the decisions made about how local health budgets are allocated. Her angry words may sound persuasive, but the law would not support her claim.

References

1 http://news.bbc.co.uk/1/hi/events/nhs_at_50/special_report/123511.stm

2 http://www.nhs.uk/thenhsexplained/history1957.asp

3 http://www.soton.ac.uk/~gk/politics/medicine.htm

4 Stephen Brown LJ in R v Central Birmingham Health Authority ex p Collier (6 January 1988, unreported, available on Lexis).

5 Preamble to the Constitution of the World Health Organization as adopted by the International Health Conference, New York, 19–22 June, 1946; signed on 22 July 1946 by the representatives of 61 states (Official Records of the World Health Organization, no. 2, p. 100) and entered into force on 7 April 1948, from http://www.who.int/about/definition/en/

6 Rawls J (1972) *A Theory of Justice*. Clarendon Press, Oxford.

7 Daniels N (1981) Health care needs and distributive justice. *Philosophy and Public Affairs.* **10**: 146.

8 Daniels N (1985) Just Health Care. Cambridge Univeristy Press, Cambridge.

9 Harris J (1991) Unprincipled QALYs. *Journal of Medical Ethics.* **17**: 185.

10 http://www.chai.org.uk

11 http://www.legislation.hmso.gov.uk/acts/en/2003en43.htm

12 http://cms.hhs.gov/about/history/

CHAPTER 11

Healthcare rights

Victoria Tippett

Rights are a powerful language in healthcare. A right describes an entitlement that one person is claiming. This results in an obligation on the part of another person to fulfil that right. The philosophy of rights is a vast subject, far more detailed than is appropriate for this chapter, but an understanding of basic rights theory and the Human Rights Act 1998 is essential to modern medical practice. This chapter outlines what rights are and how they work in practice, as well as the European Convention on Human Rights and subsequent Human Rights Act. It explores how rights affect everyday clinical practice and what case law has emerged since the introduction of the Human Rights Act to guide our work in this area.

Rights

Rights are statements that allow us to protect important things in life. Rights may protect us from harm, protect our liberty, even protect our very life itself. Whilst some philosophers advocate a system of ethics based purely on rights, most see rights as one part of a larger ethical framework. To claim a right is to use a powerful linguistic tool. A right implies that there exists a duty for others to do, or refrain from doing, something. Rights can therefore be seen as something like a set of rules. A *moral* right is a claim justified by moral principles.

Rights are sometimes absolute, but usually they are claims that may be overridden by a stronger claim. They may be positive or negative. A positive right involves an obligation upon another person to actively do something. A negative right involves an obligation upon another person to avoid doing (not do) something.

Obligations

Rights and obligations go hand in hand. Obligations are duties that fall to other people because a person is claiming a right. They may also be positive or negative.

Positive obligations involve an action, whereas negative obligations involve refraining from acting.

European Convention on Human Rights

The European Convention for the Protection of Human Rights and Fundamental Freedoms (ECHR) was drawn up in 1950 as a treaty of the Council of Europe. It has been in force since 1953, initially aiming to safeguard the rights of the individual against state intervention. It followed the adoption by the United Nations General Assembly of the Universal Declaration on Human Rights in 1948. The origin of these agreements was the war crimes tribunals following World War Two, and a determination to safeguard citizens from state tyranny in the future.

The ECHR consists of principle rights that are designed to protect the citizens of the European Union. The ECHR was incorporated into UK law (as well as the national law of the other member states) on 2 October 2000. In the UK, the relevant legislation is the Human Rights Act 1998.

The Human Rights Act 1998

The ECHR had been enforceable before October 2000, but only via the European Court of Human Rights in Strasbourg. Once the ECHR was incorporated into UK law, it was possible to enforce the Convention in courts within the UK.

One part of the Human Rights Act states that it is unlawful for a public authority to act in any way that is incompatible with the ECHR (i.e. which contravenes one of the rights of the ECHR).

In the healthcare setting, this means that NHS trusts, primary care trusts and any contractor (including dentists, GPs, opticians and pharmacists) undertaking NHS work must not act in a way that contravenes the ECHR. For this reason a working knowledge of the ECHR is essential for healthcare professionals.

Once all domestic remedies have been exhausted, i.e. the original case in the UK has been lost, the appeal case has been lost and the case at the High Court has also been lost, it is still possible to apply to the Court of Human Rights in Strasbourg. However, if *it* dismisses the case, there is no right of appeal to the Court of Human Rights.

The following pages outline the Act and briefly explain each article.

Article 1
This article states that the 'High Contracting Parties' (governors of the countries covered by the Act) give the rights and freedoms listed below to all those within their jurisdiction.

Part I: The Convention – Rights and Freedoms

Article 2   **The right to life**
This article renders the taking of life unlawful, except where it results from the use of necessary force to defend someone from unlawful violence, lawfully arrest or detain someone, or to lawfully take action to quell a riot or insurrection.

Article 3   **The prohibition of torture**
This article prohibits torture, inhuman or degrading treatment or punishment. Examples include: beating the soles of prisoners' feet, electric shock treatment and mock executions.

Article 4   **Prohibition of slavery and forced labour**
This article is self-explanatory, but specifically excludes military service or any work that is deemed part of normal civic service.

Article 5   **Right to liberty and security**
This article ensures liberty and security of a person except for procedures involving the arrest and detention of those acting unlawfully.

Article 6   **Right to a fair trial**
This article includes the right of any person charged with a criminal offence to be presumed innocent until proven guilty.

Article 7   **No punishment without law**
This oddly worded article refers to people only being convicted of crimes if the action concerned was unlawful at the time that the act took place. It prevents the retrospective application of new laws to old actions.

Article 8   **Right to respect for private and family life**
This article ensures everyone has privacy of his or her family life, home and correspondence. This right can be overridden if it is in the interests of national security, public safety, a country's economic welfare, preventing disorder or for the protection of health, morals or the rights and freedoms of other individuals.

Article 9   **Freedom of thought, conscience and religion**
This article includes the freedom to practise a religion or to change your religion. It may be overridden in most of the ways described for Article 8.

Article 10 **Freedom of expression**
This freedom may be curtailed in the interests of national security, public safety, a country's economic welfare, preventing disorder or for the protection of health, morals or the rights and freedoms of other individuals.

Article 11 **Freedom of assembly and association**
This article gives the right to peaceful assembly and association with others, including the right to form and join trade unions.

Article 12 **The right to marry**
This article gives men and women of marriageable age the right to marry and found a family, in accordance with their country's national laws. It regards the right to marry and found a family as one right. This does not include the right to divorce in order to remarry. This article was designed to protect citizens from arbitrary sterilisation or population control measures being imposed by the state. It does not guarantee single persons the right to have children out of wedlock. This is because the two elements are regarded as one right.

Article 13 **The right to an effective remedy**
This article states that those whose rights and freedoms under this Act are violated must have an effective remedy (i.e. be able to seek justice through the legal system of the country concerned), even if the person committing the violation was acting in an official capacity. (This article is present in the Council of Europe's Convention for the Protection of Human Rights and Fundamental Freedoms, but not in the Human Rights Act 1998).[1,2]

Article 14 **The prohibition of discrimination**
This article states that the rights and freedoms set out in the Convention shall be given to all citizens, with no discrimination on the basis of any ground. Examples listed include sex, race, language, social origin, property or birth status.

Article 15 allows countries to act in ways contrary to their obligations under the Convention in times of war or other public emergency.
   Articles 16, 17 and 18 outline the application of the above rights.

Part II : The First Protocol

Article 1 **The protection of property**
This article ensures that nobody is deprived of their possessions unless it is in the public interest.

Article 2   **Right to education**
The article states that nobody should be denied the right to education and that the State should respect the right of parents to educate their children in line with their own religious and philosophical convictions.

Article 3   **Right to free elections**
This ensures that the state holds free elections at reasonable intervals in time by secret ballot, and that these elections allow free expression of the opinion of the people.

Part III: The Sixth Protocol

Article 1   **Abolition of the death penalty**
Nobody should be condemned to the death penalty or executed.

Article 2   **Death penalty in time of war**
States are allowed to make exceptions for acts committed in time of war or a time when there is an imminent threat of war. The circumstances in which the death penalty would be used must be clearly laid out by the state and must be communicated to the Secretary General of the Council of Europe.

Case law

Little case law involving the Human Rights Act 1998 is available. The following are examples of UK cases involving the European Convention on Human Rights, showing how the law works in practice.

Article 2   **The Diane Pretty case**
Diane Pretty was suffering from motor neurone disease and wished to end her own life. Due to her illness she would have had to have help in this from her husband as she was not physically capable of committing suicide. Under UK law he would then have been charged for assisting her suicide. She went to court to argue that her inability to end her own life without breaking UK law contravened Articles 2 and 3 of the ECHR. Both the UK courts and the European Court of Human Rights ruled against Mrs Pretty. The final ruling in Strasbourg was on 29 April 2002 and explained that Articles 2 and 3 were aimed at the protection and preservation of life and the dignity of death, and that this did not encompass a patient having a right to their own death. Mrs Pretty died as a result of her disease a few weeks after this ruling.[3]

Articles 3 and 13 **Child protection**
In the case *Z & others v UK*,[4] breaches of Article 3 and 13 were found to have occurred. The case was brought on behalf of four children, against the local authority. The children had been abused and neglected by their parents for several years and it was argued that the local authority failed in its positive duty to protect the children from inhuman and degrading treatment. The court found that the local authority were in contravention of Article 3 (the prohibition of torture, inhuman or degrading treatment or punishment). It was also argued that the children had been denied an effective remedy in respect of their complaints. It was ruled that this did contravene Article 13. Substantial damages were awarded to each applicant (child) as a result of this case.

Article 5 **Mental health review tribunals**
A case from 2001[5] held that the previous requirement for patients to demonstrate to a mental health review tribunal that they were no longer suffering from a mental health disorder was too restrictive on patients' right to liberty (Article 5). The service provider (usually mental health trust) is now required to show that a patient is still suffering from a mental health disorder; thus the burden of proof shifts from the patient to the institution detaining them under the Mental Health Act.

 # Where you stand

- The Human Rights Act 1998 makes the ECHR enforceable in UK courts.
- Of particular relevance to medicine are the right to respect for private and family life, and the right to marry and found a family.
- This area of medical law is moving fast at the moment – you need to be aware of new developments as they occur.

 # Where you fall

- All public authorities, including NHS trusts and primary care trusts, must not act in a way that contravenes the ECHR.
- As an individual, if you contravene the Human Rights Act 1998 you may be tried and punished by a UK court or the European Court of Human Rights in Strasbourg.

Cases

> I work in a fertility clinic which does not offer treatment to lesbian couples. Does this contravene Part I Article 12 of the European Convention on Human Rights?

A decision not to offer a lesbian woman fertility treatment does not contravene Part I Article 12, her right to marry and found a family. The European Convention on Human Rights regards this article as representing one right, 'to marry and found a family', rather than as 'the right to marry' and 'the right to found a family'. This means that unmarried persons do not have the right to have children.

Article 12 also specifies that it is a *man and a woman* of marriageable age who have the right to marry and found a family. The right therefore does not apply to lesbian couples.

> I am a GP in Birmingham, and one of my patients has recently been diagnosed with human immunodeficiency virus (HIV) which she contracted whilst involved in an extramarital affair. She refuses to tell her husband of the diagnosis or to use barrier contraception. I am also her husband's GP and within the scope of the GMC guidelines I feel I must tell her husband about the diagnosis in order to protect him from harm. If I tell her husband, will I contravene Section 1 Article 8 of the European Convention on Human Rights – her right to respect for private and family life?

No, you would not contravene Section 1 Article 8, because you are acting to protect the health of another individual (i.e. her husband). You can therefore override her right to respect for private and family life under Article 8.

Within the GMC guidance is the recommendation that if your patient absolutely refuses to tell her husband you should inform her that you are going to tell him yourself and explain exactly why you feel disclosure is necessary.

References

1   http://conventions.coe.int/treaty/en/treaties/word/005.doc

2   http://www.hmso.gov.uk/acts/acts1998/19980042.htm

3   *R v DPP, ex parte Diane Pretty & Secretary of State for the Home Department (interested party) (18 October 2001)* and Application No. 2346/02 to European Court of Human Rights from http://www.dh.gov.uk/PolicyAndGuidance/equalityAndDiversity/EqualityAnd DiversityArticle/fs/en?CONTENT_ID=4054188&chk=XBC6cb

4 From http://www.dh.gov.uk/PolicyAndGuidance/equalityAndDiversity/EqualityAnd
   DiversityArticle/fs/en?CONTENT_ID=4054188&chk=XBC6cb

5 *R v Mental Health review tribunal, ex parte H* from http://www.doh.gov.uk/humanrights/
   casestudies.htm

CHAPTER 12

The new genetics

Victoria Tippett

Our genetic code is a unique set of instructions, a sort of blueprint for our growth and development that both fascinates and frightens in equal measure. Whilst most genetic techniques remain at an experimental stage of development, their potential implications for medicine and society at large are immense. This chapter explores the ethical and legal issues surrounding the 'new genetics'. From discussing the ethical basis of gene therapy and challenging our definitions of normal to comparing somatic with germline therapy and analysing cloning, the chapter explains how we can focus our genetic expertise on patient-centred care. With discussion of both individual genetic counselling and population genetic screening, the practical uses of the 'new genetics' are highlighted along with its implications for every member of society.

What is normal?

Gene therapy involves manipulation of the genes of existing or future persons. It allows us to correct abnormalities in an effort to prevent human suffering, yet in so doing it raises fundamental questions about what constitutes suffering and how we define a normal human being.

Extremes of the scale are easy to define. Few would prevent those who have inherited a genetic mutation resulting in cystic fibrosis undergoing gene therapy to allow them to lead a life free from enzyme supplements, regular physiotherapy and frequent hospital admissions. However, most would feel that using gene therapy to change the colour of a child's hair as their parents fear they would be teased at school would not be justified. If the ends of the scale are easy to define, why is the area in between so difficult? Most of it hinges on our inability to define normal. If a consensus could be reached as to what constitutes a normal human person then treatment to correct abnormalities could be carried out to avoid suffering and harm.

The World Health Organization (WHO) states that 'Health is a state of complete physical, mental and social well-being and not merely the absence of disease or infirmity'.[1] If harm is caused whenever one's health needs are not met, an argument could be made for virtually any treatment to be carried out in order to prevent suffering.

Is the important issue therefore what constitutes a person? Ethicists have long argued about what constitutes a person. This is not in the anthropological or physical sense, but what it is that distinguishes a person and makes them special in moral terms, allowing differences in their treatment from, say, chimpanzees or dolphins. One argument, put forward by John Harris, centres on the person being able to value their own life.[2] It follows that if you can value your life, you can express feelings regarding the continuation or termination of that life.

So what is it about personhood that is special?

As people we have the ability to plan future action and to consider consequences of action now upon our future life. This has been cited as one of the main abilities that separates us from much of the animal kingdom, who seem to act on 'animal instinct' and live from moment to moment. It is therefore argued that creatures who have no concept of themselves existing in the future lose nothing by having that future denied them. It is the frustration of our hopes and plans for the future that causes our suffering if that future is cut short.*

If it is the acquisition of personhood that gives us important rights to our continued existence, the point at which we are said to become a person is vital. Very few commentators would argue that sperm and ova are persons and accordingly, menstruation is not seen as the death of persons (more accurately, potential persons) or as morally wrong. Given this, at what point is a person created? Is it the moment at which sperm and ovum fuse to create a zygote? Is it when the morula is formed? Is it when the embryo implants? Is it when the fetus is sufficiently mature to be able to survive (with support) if born prematurely? Is it the moment of live birth, regardless of gestation? Or is it after birth, at the point when the infant has developed a sense of self and values its own life?

It may seem to be splitting hairs to try to reach a consensus on when a person is created, but precise definition is crucial. It governs what we can carry out in terms of research on embryos and fetuses, use of fetal material (for example for stem cell transplantation), contraception and also terminations of pregnancy.

An alternative approach is to state that it is not personhood but the *potential* for personhood that is important. This allows a distinction to be drawn between fetuses in early development and animals who have many of the same

---

* This area of ethics is fascinating. Space prohibits further discussion in this chapter, but good source texts can be found in the resource section at the end of this book.

characteristics as a fetus – of functioning organs and the ability to experience pain. Such animals we experiment upon and kill to eat freely, yet such actions upon fetuses would seem grotesque to many. Is it the fetus's potential for personhood that makes it special and prohibits us from treating it like an animal?

Given that opinions vary, the law has had to come to a consensus. Chapter 7 details the law relating to reproductive assistance and abortion.

Embryo research

Under the Human Fertilisation and Embryology Act 1990, research (*in vitro*) on human embryos is not legal without a licence from the Human Fertilisation and Embryology Authority (HFEA). Two types of licence must be obtained – one covering the premises in which the research is undertaken and one covering the specific research project in question. In general, the research will be granted a licence if it can be shown that the work can *only* be undertaken on embryos, and the research increases knowledge about embryos, increases knowledge about the treatment of infertility or serious diseases or enables knowledge to be applied to treating serious diseases. The HFEA expects projects to have received ethics committee approval (see Chapter 9) and uses independent academics to assess licence applications.

Aside from the need for a licence, there are statutory requirements relating to embryo research.

- The embryos must be no more than 14 days old (after fertilisation).
- A human embryo cannot be placed into a non-human (i.e. an animal).
- The nucleus of a cell or embryo cannot be replaced.
- It is necessary for the donors whose gametes formed the embryo to consent to its use for research (after counselling).

It is also worth noting that members of staff may conscientiously object to participating in such research.

Fetal research

In 1989 the Polkinghorne Committee reviewed the guidance on Research Use of Fetuses and Fetal Material. A code of practice was issued following this review. This governs fetuses and fetal material but not placental tissue. If written consent is obtained from the mother, the fetus or fetal tissue may be used for research. It is stressed that the mother must have decided to terminate the pregnancy before the possibility of research is suggested, so that there is no risk of fetuses being terminated just to facilitate research. If a spontaneous abortion occurs, only once the fetus has died may consent be sought for its use in research.

This code of practice is used by ethics committees when deciding whether to approve research. The committee must also be satisfied that the research can *only* be undertaken on fetuses and that the researchers involved possess the necessary skills and equipment to carry it out.

Gene therapy

The government set up the Human Genetics Commission (HGC) in 1999 to advise ministers on the way human genetics was developing and its implications for their policies. It particularly focuses on legal, ethical, healthcare and economic implications of human genetics. Its members represent experts in their field and cover areas of law, bioethics, medicine, nursing and clinical genetics.

In addition to the research ethics committees discussed in Chapter 9, specific committees have been set up to consider gene therapy and xenotransplantation (see Chapter 6). The Gene Therapy Advisory Committee (GTAC) was set up by the Department of Health. This was established in 1993 to advise on how ethically acceptable proposals for human gene therapy research are and to inform ministers regarding current developments in gene therapy research.

The new genetics and patients

Genetic counselling

Genetic counselling provides patients with access to a skilled professional to give them information and non-directional counselling as they make important decisions about whether to undergo genetic testing and, where applicable, what form of testing to have. A lot of the discussion will centre on probabilities, based on the patient or patient's family history, and a skilled counsellor will tailor the discussion to the particular patient and their information needs.

It is vital that whenever a patient is offered genetic testing there is counselling to go along with the test and to support patients. Pre-test counselling is particularly important, so that patients can decide how much information they want and what they will want to do with their news. It allows patients to talk through their options depending on the outcome of the test, so that they do not find themselves overwhelmed once the results are available.

Genetic screening

Where genetic counselling focuses on risk to the individual, genetic screening targets risk amongst a population.

To be effective, a screening test should meet the WHO Criteria for Screening, drawn up by Wilson and Jungner in 1968:

- condition you are screening for is an important health problem
- natural history of the condition is well understood
- condition has a detectable early stage
- treatment for the condition at an early stage should be more effective than at a later stage
- a suitable and valid test for the early stage should be available
- that test should be acceptable to patients
- there should be determined intervals at which to repeat the test
- the health service should have the necessary resources to deal with the increase in clinical workload resulting from the screening tests
- the benefits should outweigh the risks
- the benefits should outweigh the costs.[3]

In the case of genetic screening tests the 'detectable early stage' equates to the presence of the genetic abnormality and the ability to detect it. Some genetic screening tests have been proposed as meeting these criteria. One example is cystic fibrosis. A genetic test can be carried out at birth, but it is currently only performed by most centres on selected infants identified as being at risk of the disease. If the test could be shown to be acceptable and cost-effective, it could be used to screen the population at large for cystic fibrosis. The key motivation for genetic screening is early detection and treatment of the disease in question to minimise its morbidity and mortality.

Gene therapy techniques

Somatic versus germline gene therapy

Gene therapy may be somatic (involving any cell in the body except sperm or ova) or germline (involving sperm and ova). Somatic therapy aims to treat an existing person. This is often achieved via the insertion of genetic material that the person lacks, for example the gene necessary to produce a specific protein. Germline therapy usually involves inserting genetic material into the sperm or ova of an individual. Whilst this will not directly affect the patient under-going the insertion of the material, it will affect their future children. It could, therefore, be used to eliminate undesirable characteristics or add in desirable characteristics to future children. Despite these techniques still being at the research stage, they have given rise to massive international public debate. It has even been suggested that such research should not be allowed to proceed.

The Clothier Committee in 1992 and the Group of Advisors on Ethical Implications of Biotechnology of the European Commission in 1994 examined the ethics of somatic gene therapy and found it to be ethically unproblematic. Somatic gene therapy was likened to any other form of treatment that an individual may receive such as surgery or a medicine. Trials are currently underway involving somatic gene therapy for conditions such as cystic fibrosis, cancer and auto immune deficiency syndrome (AIDS).[4]

Germline therapy has proved more controversial. It has the capacity to affect people who do not yet exist and it is this effect on the future that prompts debate. In some cases there is little room for disagreement. Where the genetic manipulation prevents the transmission of a disease from parent to child, few would object. However, many fear that this would open the door to parents choosing to eliminate characteristics that are not harmful but may be seen as socially undesirable, such as the wrong colour hair or eyes. This concept is described by some ethicists as the 'slippery slope' argument. Allowing germline therapy to prevent serious diseases, putting a foot on the top of our slippery slope, leads us to slide down that slope to germline therapy for protruding ears or ginger hair, if parents were to perceive these as undesirable characteristics.

Other ethicists do not subscribe to the slippery slope argument, proposing that the application of ethical crampons before setting foot on a slippery slope allows you to descend only so far as you wish, and to descend safely. Allowing germline therapy to prevent serious diseases does not necessarily lead to therapy for cosmetic reasons.

The argument has raged for 10 years or more and yet there is still no consensus. Do we forbid all such germline work in order that eugenically motivated individuals cannot abuse the technology or can we hold on to a demarcation between eugenic and therapeutic gene therapy? The discussion continues on an international scale.

Cloning

Cloning involves the production of an exact genetic double of a living organism. The most famous clone is, of course, Dolly the sheep. She was born in 1997, having been created by taking a nucleus from an adult sheep and fusing it with an unfertilised egg whose nucleus had been removed. Another adult sheep then carried the egg for a normal gestation.

Why clone?

Cloning technology allows us to take cells from embryos and dead fetuses and use them to make pluripotent cell lines. This has the potential to allow the growth of replacement cells and tissues for patients who suffer from disease of a particular body part. This has massive positive implications for diseases such as Parkinson's disease, where it is hoped that dopaminergic neurones could be grown and transplanted to treat the condition. The more daunting potential of this technology is the creation of entire human clones. It would allow an adult to create children who share the exact same genetic make-up as themselves.

Ethicists worry about two key concepts. The first is that children may be created as spare-part reservoirs for their parents, as their tissues would all be an exact tissue match if transplantation were needed. The second is that creating an exact genetic copy of a person somehow challenges our concepts of what it is to be human and what makes an individual unique. The first area of concern could be dealt with by careful legislation. The second area is more problematic, but it should be remembered that whilst parent and child would be genetically the same, they would not be the same person. Our genetic self interacts with the environment to produce our phenotype – how our genes are expressed as a person. The child would therefore be similar to the parent but not the 'carbon copy' that some members of the public fear will be created.

Cloning law

In the UK, Parliament voted in 2000 to legalise the creation of embryos purely for research purposes, including for stem cell research. It has also been decided that a cloned human is an 'embryo' for the purposes of the Human Fertilisation and Embryology Act 1990. This means that it is unlikely that licences allowing cloning as a means of human reproduction will be granted by the HFEA. However, it remains unclear how long an outright ban on reproduction cloning can remain in place. This is certainly an area of medical law and ethics that merits careful observation for rapid new developments in the years to come.

 Where you stand

- *In vitro* research on human embryos requires a licence from the HFEA for both the research premises and the specific research project.
- You may conscientiously object to participating in embryo research.
- Any patient offered genetic testing should be given pre-test counselling.
- Embryos may be created purely for research testing.

Where you fall

- For embryo research the embryos must be no more than 14 days post fertilisation.
- A human embryo cannot be placed into a non-human (animal).
- The nucleus of a cell or embryo cannot be replaced.
- The donors of gametes used to form embryos must consent to the use of the embryo for research purposes (after appropriate counselling).
- Consent to use fetal tissue cannot be obtained until *after* the mother has decided to terminate the pregnancy or, in cases of spontaneous abortion, until after the fetus has died.
- Unlicensed research is highly unlikely to be published and is illegal – you could run the risk of prosecution.

Cases

I am a Senior House Officer (SHO) in paediatrics. One of our patients has been diagnosed with cystic fibrosis. My consultant wants me to ask the parents to consent to genetic testing of the child and his siblings. Help! How do I do this?

This is not an easy task and if you do not feel happy holding such a conversation with these parents, you should turn to your seniors for support and assistance. Find out whether your hospital has a genetic counselling service. If so, after some preliminary discussion, it would probably be appropriate to refer the family to them for formal counselling by professionals trained in this specific area.

If you do undertake this counselling, it is important to ascertain what the parents understand about the condition and how it comes about – i.e. the basic genetics involved in cystic fibrosis transmission – and fill in any gaps in their knowledge. This may be a good opportunity to talk to them about their family history – has anybody else in the family got cystic fibrosis or symptoms suggestive of it? It is next important to explain what is actually involved in the test on a practical level, and which family members should be tested.

Then, the implications of the test results should be explained and explored with the family. How much information would they want? Have they discussed this with other family members who may be affected such as the child's aunts, uncles and grandparents? It is then important to talk about what the family may choose to do with the information gained from genetic testing.

In most cases, whilst as an SHO you will be able to have preliminary discussions with this family, senior or specialist help will almost certainly be needed before the tests are undertaken.

> I work as a junior doctor in neurology and my team has just diagnosed Huntington's disease in a 56-year-old man. He is aware of his diagnosis. How do I approach the subject of genetic testing for his family with him?

This sort of discussion should not take place without senior support – preferably that of your consultant. Firstly, check the patient's understanding of the disease and how it is inherited. Fill in any gaps but remember to keep your explanations of genetics simple. Good analogies are to betting or gambling – many people will understand chance or odds better than percentage risk. Diagrams and family trees can also be useful.

The next step is to ask the patient if he wants his relatives to know his diagnosis. If not, it would be impossible to test his relatives. You could argue that you ought to persuade him to let you disclose his diagnosis to his family members so that they could be tested, but as there is no cure and little treatment for the condition there are not compelling reasons in favour of disclosure against his will.

If he agrees to your discussing the diagnosis with them, this must be conducted very sensitively. After a basic explanation it is important to ascertain whether or not they wish to have further information or undergo genetic testing. If they decide not to, you must respect that decision and not attempt to force information upon them that they do not wish to have.

The key issues with Huntington's disease are its late onset after many symptom-free years and the lack of a cure or effective treatment. The main benefit to testing is for young family members contemplating starting a family, who may decide against having children if they know they would pass on the gene for Huntington's disease.

With this area you should, as far as possible, attempt to contact a specialist organization used to offering genetic counselling and dealing with the issues surrounding Huntington's disease specifically, for example the Huntington's Disease Association http://www.hda.org.uk/

References

1 Preamble to the Constitution of the World Health Organization as adopted by the International Health Conference, New York, 19–22 June, 1946; signed on 22 July 1946 by the representatives of 61 states (Official Records of the World Health Organization, no. 2, p. 100) and entered into force on 7 April 1948, from http://www.who.int/about/definition/en/

2 Harris J (1985) *The Value of Life*. Routledge & Kegan Paul, London.

3 http://education.med.ic.ac.uk/Year/5th/EPH/EPH-revision02.doc

4 http://www.aegis.com/aaidsline/1999/mar/

Resources

Print

- *Confidentiality: protecting and providing information.*
  Booklet produced by the General Medical Council.

- *Good Medical Practice.*
  Booklet produced by the General Medical Council.

- *Seeking Patients' Consent: the ethical considerations.*
  Booklet produced by the General Medical Council.

- *Confidentiality.*
  Booklet produced by the General Medical Council.

- *Research: the role and responsibilities of doctors.*
  Booklet produced by the General Medical Council.

- *Reference Guide to Consent for Examination or Treatment.*
  Department of Health from http://www.doh.gov.uk

- 'The Protection and Use of Patient Information: Guidance from the Department of Health.' Section 4.9 at http://www.doh.gov.uk

- *Good Practice in Consent Implementation Guide: consent to examination or treatment.*
  Department of Health from http://www.doh.gov.uk

- Beauchamp TL and Childress JF (1994) *Principles of Biomedical Ethics.* Oxford University Press, Oxford.

- Branthwaite M (2000) *Law for Doctors: principles and practicalities.* Royal Society of Medicine Press, London.

- Brazier M (1992) *Medicine, Patients and the Law.* Penguin, London.

- Campbell A, Charlesworth M, Gillett G *et al.* (1997) *Medical Ethics.* Oxford University Press, Oxford.

- Conference of Medical Colleges and Faculties of the United Kingdom (1988) *Working Party on Organ Transplantation in Neonates*. DHSS, London.

- Consensus statement by teachers of medical ethics and law in UK medical schools (1998) Teaching medical ethics and law within medical education: a model for the UK core curriculum. *Journal of Medical Ethics*. **24**: 188–92.

- Daniels N (1981) Health-care needs and distributive justice. *Philosophy & Public Affairs*. **10**: 146.

- Delhanty J, Wells DA, Dagan H *et al.*(1997) Genetic diagnosis before implantation. *BMJ*. **315**: 828–9.

- Doyal L and Gillon R (1998) Medical ethics and law as core subject material in medical education (editorial). *BMJ*. **316**: 1623–4.

- Dyer C (1992) Boy wins damages after injury in utero. *BMJ*. **304**: 1400.

- Dyson A and Harris J (eds) (1990) *Experiments on Embryos*. Routledge, London.

- Fears R, Roberts D and Poste G (2000) Rational or rationed medicine? The promise of genetics for improved clinical practice. *BMJ*. **320**: 933–5.

- Fortin J (1998) *Children's Rights and the Developing Law*. Butterworth, London.

- Foster C (2001) *The Ethics of Medical Research on Humans*. Cambridge University Press, Cambridge.

- Frey RG and Paton W (1983) Vivisection, morals and medicine: an exchange. *Journal of Medical Ethics*. **9**: 94–7 and 102–4.

- Gillon R (1992) *Philosophical Medical Ethics*. John Wiley & Sons, Chichester.

- Goodman N (2000) Rational rationing. *BMJ*. **321**: 1356.

- Harris J (1985) *The Value of Life*. Routledge & Kegan Paul, London.

- Harris J (1991) Unprincipled QALYs. *Journal of Medical Ethics*. **17**: 185.

- Harris J and Holm S (eds) (1998) *The Future of Human Reproduction*. Clarendon Press, Oxford.

- Hope T, Savulescu J and Hendrick J (2003) *Medical Ethics and Law: the core curriculum*. Churchill Livingstone, Edinburgh.

- Josefson D (1998) News: breast cancer trial stopped early. *BMJ*. **316**: 1185.

- Leckie D and Pickersgill D (1999) *The 1998 Human Rights Act Explained*. The Stationery Office, London.

- Leung W (2000) *Law for Doctors*. Blackwell Science, Oxford.

- Levine R J (1986) *Ethics and Regulation of Clinical Research*. Urban & Schwarzenberg, Baltimore.

- Mason JK, McCall Smith RA and Laurie GT (2002) *Law and Medical Ethics*. Butterworths, London.

- Maynard A and Sheldon T (2001) Limits to demand for health care. *BMJ*. **322**: 734.

- McHale J, Fox M and Murphy J (1997) *Health Care Law: text and materials*. Sweet & Maxwell, London.

- Midgley M (1983) *Animals and Why They Matter*. Penguin, Harmondsworth, Middlesex.

- Montgomery J (2002) *Health Care Law*. Oxford University Press, Oxford.

- Morgan D (2001) *Issues in Medical Law and Ethics*. Cavendish Publishing, London.

- Rawlins M (2001) The failings of NICE. *BMJ*. **322**: 489.

- Rawls J (1972) *A Theory of Justice*. Clarendon Press, Oxford.

- Regan T (1983) *The Case for Animal Rights*. Berkley, New York.

- Regan T and Singer P (1989) *Animal Rights and Human Obligations*. Lawrence Erlbaum, Englewood Cliffs, New Jersey.

- RCP (1997) *Royal College of Physicians Guidelines on the Practice of Ethical Committees in Medical Research involving Human Subjects*. Royal College of Physicians, London. publications@rcplondon.ac.uk

- Whitfield A (1993) Common law duties to unborn children. *Medical Law Review*. **1**: 28.

- Wiggins D (1991) *Needs, Values, Truth*. Blackwell, Oxford.

- Winslade W (1981) Surrogate mothers: private right or public wrong? *Journal of Medical Ethics*. **7**: 153.

Electronic

- http://adc.bmjjournals.com/cgi/content/full/archdischild%3b82/2/177?maxtoshow=%3feaf

- http://www.aegis.com/aidsline/1999/mar/a9930001.html

- http://www.bmj.bmjjournals.com/cgi/content/full/328/7434/246-a

- http://adc.bmjjournals.com/cgi/content/full/archdischild%3b82/2/177? maxtoshow=%3feaf

- http://www.bma.org.uk/ap.nsf/Content/Duty+of+candour

- http://www.bma.org.uk/ap.nsf/Content/pas+project+-+select+ ctteereports

- http://www.bma.org.uk/public/ethics.nsf/fafbe9dab4bd8b18802566 a600346bef/df487b1e0e618f30802566a6003d304a?OpenDocument# Conscientious_0

- https://www.britcoun.org.uk/governance/jusrig/human/echr/

- http://www.chai.org.uk

- http://cms.hhs.gov/about/history/

- http://conventions.coe.int/treaty/en/Treaties/Word/005.doc

- http://www.corec.org.uk

- http://www.corec.org.uk/standardform.htm

- *R v DPP, ex parte Diane Pretty & Secretary of State for the Home Department (inter- ested party) (18 October 2001)* and Application No. 2346/02 to European Court of Human Rights from http://www.dh.gov.uk/PolicyAndGuidance/ equalityAndDiversity/EqualityAndDiversityArticle/fs/en?CONTENT_ID= 4054188&chk=XBC6cb

- http://www.doh.gov.uk/complain.htm

- http://www.doh.gov.uk/genetics/gtac/index.htm

- http://www.doh.gov.uk/genetics/whitepaper.htm

- http://www.doh.gov.uk/humanrights/casestudies.htm

- http://www.doh.gov.uk/humanrights/lac0017.htm

- http://www.doh.gov.uk/humanrights/qa.htm

- http://www.doh.gov.uk/nhsplan/npch3.htm

- http://www.doh.gov.uk/nice/index.htm

- http://www.doh.gov.uk/ukxira

- http://education.med.ic.ac.uk/Year/5th/EPH/EPH-revision02.doc

- http://www.elsevier-international.com/e-books/pdf/217.pdf

- http://www.gig.org.uk

- http://www.gmc-uk.org/med_ed/meded_frameset.htm
- http://www.gmc-uk.org/probdocs/default.htm
- http://www.gmc-uk.org/standards/research.htm
- http://www.gmc-uk.org/standards/secret.htm
- http://www.gmc-uk.org/standards/standards_frameset.htm
- http://www.hda.org.uk/
- http://www.hfea.gov.uk/
- http://www.hfea.gov.uk/PressOffice/Archive/1068631271
- http://www.hfea.gov.uk/PressOffice/Backgroundpapers/DonorAnonymity
- http://www.hgc.gov.uk
- http://www.hgc.gov.uk/genesdirect/index.htm
- http://www.hmso.gov.uk/acts/acts1990/Ukpga_19900037_en_1.htm
- http://www.hmso.gov.uk/acts/acts1998/19980042.htm
- http://medicines.mhra.gov.uk/ourwork/licensingmeds/types/clintrialdir.htm#impuk
- http://mrc.ac.uk/index/current-research/current-clinical_research/funding-clinical_research_governance/current-eu_clinical_trials_directive.htm
- http://www.mrc.ac.uk/pdf-htb.views.updated_25jun04.pdf
- http://news.bbc.co.uk/1/hi/events/nhs_at_50/special_report/123511.stm
- http://news.bbc.co.uk/hi/english/health/newsid_954000/954408.stm
- http://www.nhs.uk/nationalplan/
- http://www.nhs.uk/nhsmagazine/primarycare/archives/sept2003/feature5.asp
- http://www.nhs.uk/nhsmagazine/story2716.asp
- http://www.nhs.uk/retainedorgans/
- http://www.nhs.uk/orgs/doh/news/2001/april/231/asp
- http://www.nhs.uk/thenhsexplained/history1957.asp
- http://www.publications.parliament.uk/pa/cm200304/cmbills/049/2004049.htm

- http://www.rcog.org.uk/guidelines.asp?PageID=108&GuidelineID=26
- http://www.scotland.gov.uk/about/JD/CL/00016360/medres.aspx
- http://www.soton.ac.uk/~gk/politics/medicine.htm
- http://www.wma.net/e/policy/b3.htm

Cases

A v C (1985) **8** *Fam Law*: 170 per Ormrod LJ.

A-G's Reference (No 3 of 1994) (1996) **2** *All ER*: 10, (1998) **1** *Cr App Rep* 91, HL.

Airedale NHS Trust v Bland (1993) **1** *All ER*: 821.

Bolam v Friern Management Committee (1957) **2** *All ER*: 118 at 121.

Butler Sloss LJ in Re MB (Caesarean Section) Times 18th April 1997 Court of Appeal.

Canterbury v Spence (1972) **464** *F 2d*: 727 DC.

Hunter v Mann (1974) **1** *QB*: 767 at 772.

Lord Woolfe MR in *Pearce v United Bristol Healthcare NHS Trust* (1999) **48** *BMLR*: 118.

Paton v British Pregnancy Advisory Service Trustees (1978) **2** *All ER*: 987.

R v Bourne (1939) **1** *KB*: 687.

R v Bournewood Community and Mental Health Trust ex parte L (1998) **2** *FLR*: 550.

R v Central Birmingham Health Authority ex p Collier (6 January 1988, unreported, available on Lexis).

R v Human Fertilisation and Embryology Authority, ex p Blood (1997) **2** *All ER*: 687, (1997) **35** *BMLR*: 1, CA.

R v Secretary of State for Health, ex p Pfizer Ltd (1999) *Lloyd's Rep Med*: 289, (2000) **51** *BMLR*: 189.

R v Smith (1974) **1** *All ER*: 376.

Re C (adult refusal of medical treatment) (1994) **1** *All ER*: 819 at 824.

Re F (mental patient: sterilisation) (1990) **2** *AC*: 1, sub nom F v West Berkshire Health Authority (1989) **2** *All ER*: 545.

Re J (a minor) (wardship: medical treatment) (1992) **4** *All ER*: 614.

Re MB (an adult: medical treatment) (1997) **2** *FLR*: 426.

Re S (a minor) (medical treatment) (1994) **2** *FLR*: 1065.

Re W (a minor) (medical treatment: court's jurisdiction) (1993) *Fam*: 64.

Re Y (adult patient) (transplant: bone marrow) (1997) **35** *MLR*: 111.

Riverside Mental Health NHS Trust v Fox (1993) **20** *BMLR*: 1.

Sidaway v Board of Governors of Bethlem Royal Hospital (1984) *AC*: 871 at 903.

Thake v Maurice (1986) *QB*: 644.

Statutes and bills

The Abortion Act 1967

The Access to Health Records Act 1990

The Access to Medical Reports Act 1988

The Anatomy Act 1984

The Birth and Death Registration Act 1953

The Children Act 1989

The Congenital Disabilities (Civil Liberty) Act 1976

The Data Protection Act 1984 and 1998

The Family Law Reform Act 1969

The Human Fertilisation and Embryology Act 1990

The Human Organ Transplants Act 1989

The Human Rights Act 1998

The Human Tissue Act 1961

The Human Tissue Act (Northern Ireland) 1962

The Human Tissue Bill (not yet law)

The Medical Act 1858

The Mental Health Act 1959

The Mental Health Act 1983

The Misuse of Drugs Act (Notification of Supply to Addict) Regulation 1973

The National Health Service Act 1977

The Public Health (Control of Disease) Act 1984

The Surrogacy Arrangements Act 1985

Appendix

The Adults with Incapacity (Scotland) Act 2000 Section 51

http://www.scotland-legislation.hmso.gov.uk/legislation/scotland/ssi2002/20020190.htm

Adults with incapacity may want to participate in medical or other research, to help in the search for more knowledge about the illness and diagnosis, treatment and prevention. However, their consent must not be taken for granted. Some people will be able to take such decisions for themselves and may be able to consent to research. They may wish to indicate their general willingness to participate in research by making an advance statement to say so or by granting someone a welfare power of attorney with the power to consent to research on their behalf. The new Act sets out clear rules for what medical, surgical, psychological, nursing or dental research can be done using people who cannot consent.

Under the Act, research involving people unable to consent to take part can only be done if it could not be carried out with people who can consent. The research must be about the cause, diagnosis, care or treatment of the person's illness. It must be likely to produce a 'real and substantial benefit' for the person or to bring understanding that will help other people with the same condition.

The research must be approved by a special Ethics Committee and must involve no more than minimal foreseeable risk or discomfort. The adult should be withdrawn from the research immediately if at any time he or she objects in any way or appears to suffer discomfort.

The research cannot involve anyone who is unwilling to take part. The researchers must get consent from the person's welfare attorney or guardian, if there is one, or else from the nearest relative. If it is not possible to get this consent, it will not be legal for the adult to participate.

http://www.scotland.gov.uk/about/JD/CL/00016360/medres.aspx

Index

Page numbers in italics refer to tables or flow charts

abortion   74–5
   allowed circumstances   74–5
   and conscientious objection   74–5, 77–8
   emergency procedures   75
   later than 24 weeks   75, 76
   legislation   74
   position of fathers   75
   reporting duties   21
   under-age pregnancies and Gillick
      competence   30–1, 36
Access to Health Records Act 1990   22–3
Access to Medical Reports Act 1988   22
advance directives   53–4, 60–1
Airedale NHS Trust v Bland (1993)   50
alcohol abuse, and healthcare
      rationing   118
Alder Hey enquiry   102
Anatomy Act   1984   102
animals
   in medical research   102, 136
   and xenotransplantation   55
anorexia nervosa, and treatment
      consent   41
ARC *see* Assessment Review Committee
      (ARC) proceedings
Area Child Protection Committee (ACPC)
      procedures   33
Assessment Review Committee (ARC)
      proceedings   84, 86–7
assisted suicide   47, 53, 61
autonomy   1–2

'basic care', defined   47
'basic need', defined   114
Blood, Diane   72
Bolam principle   4, 11

R v Bournewood Community and Mental
      Health Trust ex parte (1998)   38
   breaking bad news
   patient's right to refuse information   4–5
   withholding information from patients
      3–6
British Medical Association, on patient
      rights to information   4–5

Re C (adult refusal of medical treatment)
      (1994)   40
caesarean section   66–7, 78
   consent refusal   78
cancer treatments, gamete harvesting and
      storage   71–2
Central Office for Research and Ethics
      Committees (COREC)   105
Child Assessment Order (CAO)   32
child protection
   confidentiality of patient information   21
   Emergency Protection Order (EPO)   32–3
   investigating potential abuse   31–4
   legal position   34–5, 126
   neglect/emotional abuse   34
   physical abuse   33
   sexual abuse   33–4
children
   consent to treatment   11–12, 19,
      28–31, 35–6
   concept of Gillick competence   30–1, 36
   and medical research   101
   as organ/tissue donors   57, 135
   parental responsibility   27–8, 35–6
   and *in loco parentis*   28, 35
   right to refuse treatment   30–1
   see also child protection

Children Act 1989
  child protection 32
  parents' rights 29
clinical mistakes, legal and professional
  responsibilities 90
clinical trials *see* medical research
Clinical Trials Directive (EU) 103–4
cloning 134–5
  legal position 135
Clothier Committee 134
Code of Practice on Openness in the
  NHS 23
Commission for Health Audit and Inspection
  (CHAI) 116
competency *see* patient competency;
  professional competency
complaints procedures (NHS) 92, 93
confidentiality 17–26
  basic law 17–18
  disclosure after death 20
  disclosure for education/research
    purposes 19–20
  disclosure to employers 24
  disclosure to family 25–6
  disclosure to other care providers
    18–19, 24–5
  and genetic testing 137
  judicial requests for disclosure 20, 22
  legal position 23
  patient access to health records 22–3
  patient access to medical reports 22
  penalties for breaches 23
  statutory disclosure 20–1
  sources of advice for practitioners 17
  and whistleblowing 91, 92
  see also informed consent
consent 9–16
  key components 10–12
  decisions taken by courts 12
  legal framework and position 9–10, 15
  patient competency 2, 11–12
  patient information-giving 5–7, 10–12
  patient volition 10, 13
  timing and responsibilities 13–14
  written or verbal 14
consent forms 14, 15–16
COREC *see* Central Office for Research and
  Ethics Committees
cosmetic surgery, and resource
  rationing 119

counselling services
  and genetic testing 132, 135–7
  for medical students 82–3
CPR guidelines 54, 61–2
cystic fibrosis, and genetic testing 136–7

Data Protection Act 1998 23
Declaration of Helinski 96–7
diagnosis delivery
  patient's right to refuse information 4–5
  withholding information from patients
    3–6, 25–6
Diane Blood 72
Diane Pretty 125
Disability Discrimination Act 1995 118
disciplinary proceedings *see* misconduct
DNR decisions 54, 61–2
doctor–patient communication 5–6
  see also breaking bad news; informed
    consent
doctrine of double effect 48
driving, disclosure of information to
  DVLA 24
drug misuse and treatment, disclosure of
  information 21

electronic information sources *see*
  websites
embryos
  legal status 65–6, 135, 136
  use in medical research 131, 135
emergency procedures
  abortions 75
  caesarean sections 78
  and informed consent 13
Emergency Protection Order (EPO)
  32–3
ethics committees 104–5
  see also gene therapy; medical research
EU Clinical Trials Directive 103–4
European Convention on Human Rights
  (ECHR) 122
euthanasia
  and advance directives 53–4, 60–1
  and assisted suicide 53, 61
  defined 47
  Diane Pretty case 125
  ethical arguments 51–3
  legal position 53, 125
  and resuscitation 54, 61–2

fertility treatments
  age related issues   70
  and donor anonymity   70
  donor screening   69–70
  guidelines   69–71
  legal framework   77, 127
  and reporting duties   21
  responsibility towards welfare of unborn
      child   70–1
  see also gamete storage; Human
      Fertilisation and Embryology Act
      1990; surrogacy
fetus
  legal status   65–6, 136
  use in research   131–2
France, healthcare systems   116–17

gamete storage   71–2
  and informed consent   14, 131
  length of time   72
  use of sperm/eggs from dead spouse   72
gene therapy   129–30, 132
  concepts of personhood   130–1
  and counselling   132
  donor consent   131
  and screening   67–8, 72–3, 132–3,
      136–7
  techniques   133–4
Gene Therapy Advisory Committee
    (GTAC)   132
General Medical Council   81–94
  background and structure   81–2
  on disclosure of patient information   17,
      18–20, 24
  on health problems and misconduct of
      practitioners   84–90
  on health problems and misconduct of
      students   82–3
  on medical research   98
  on patient rights to information   4
genetic testing and screening   67–8, 72–3,
    132–3, 136–7
germ-line gene therapy   133–4
Germany, healthcare systems   116–17
Gillick Competence   30–1, 36

'health', WHO definition   113, 130
health problems (doctors), GMC Health
    Committee proceedings   84, 89

health records, patient access   22–3
Health Service Commissioner, contact
    details   93
Health and Social Care Act 2003   116
healthcare rights   121–7
  European Convention on Human Rights
      (ECHR)   122
  Human Rights Act 1998   10, 65,
      122–6
Human Fertilisation and Embryology Act
    1990   69–71, 131, 135–6
  on age of donors   70
  on anonymity   70
  on donor screening   69–70
  on numbers of embryo   71
  on status of recipient couples   70
  on welfare of the child   70–1
Human Genetics Commission (HGC)   132
Human Immunodeficiency Virus (HIV),
      parental refusal for child testing   29
Human Organ Transplants Act 1989
    102
Human Rights Act 1998   10, 65,
    122–6
  case law   125–6
Human Tissue Act 1961   58, 102
Human Tissue Bill   56, 102
Huntington's Disease, and genetic
    testing   137

in loco parentis   28, 35
infertility treatment *see* fertility treatments
information sources (lists)   139–144
  see also websites
informed consent
  disclosure of information   19–20
  hospital post mortems for research
      purposes   102–3
  and mental disability   41–3, 97–8,
      100–1
  and mental illness   40–1
  and medical research   14, 19–20, 98,
      99–100, 102–3, 131
  and the right to refuse treatment   13, 16,
      30–1
  use of organs and tissues   102
  see also advance directives

Jehovah's Witnesses   29, 35

learning disabilities
  and consent to medical research 97–8,
    100–1
  and proxy consent 41–3
legal cases (lists) 145–6
legal statutes and bills (lists) 147
lesbian and gay couples, fertility
    treatments 127
licence to practice 90
life-prolonging treatment, defined 47

medical records, patient access 22–3
medical reports, patient access 22
medical research 95–109
  application procedures 105–8
  background and history 95–7
  confidentiality 14, 19–20, 98, 99–100
  ethical and legal frameworks 96–7,
    97–8
  guidance on role of doctors 98
  informed consent 14, 19–20, 98,
    99–100, 102–3, 131
  multi-centre trials 106, *108*
  stopping trials early 103, 109
  use of animals 102
  use of children 101
  use of embryos 131
  use of fetus 131–2
  use of cadavers 102–3
  use of organs and tissues 102
  use of placebos 97
  use of students and prisoners 101–2
medical students
  participating in research 101–2
  support systems 82–3
Medicare/Medicaid (USA) 116–17
mental disabilities *see* learning disabilities
Mental Health Act (MHA) 1983
  compulsory admissions *39*
  voluntary admissions 38
R v Mental Health review tribunal,
    ex parte H 126
mental health treatments
  categories of disorder 37
  compulsory admissions 38–41
  informal admissions 38
  legal position 43–4, 126
  proxy consent 41–3
  refusal of treatment 40–1

mental illness
  and consent 40–1, 41–3
  see also mental health treatments
misconduct
  Assessment Review Committee (ARC)
    proceedings 84, *86–7*
  Professional Conduct Committee (PCC)
    proceedings 84, *88*
  and the right to appeal 84, 90
  screening of cases *85*
mistakes, legal and professional
    responsibilities 90
Misuse of Drugs Act (Notification of Supply
    to Addict) Regulation 1973 21

National Institute for Clinical Excellence
    (NICE) 116
neonates
  legal status 66
  organ/tissue donation 58–9
NHS complaints procedures 92, *93*
NHS Modernisation Agency 116
Nuremberg Code 96

Organ Transplants Act 1989 56
organ/tissue donation
  with children 57
  gamete donation 70–2
  for medical research 102
  see also gene therapy; transplantation

parens patriae 30–1
parental responsibility 27–8, 35–6
  differences between parents over
    consent 29
  and *in locus parentis* 28, 35
  legal relationship between mother and
    fetus 66
paternalism 1–2, 42
patient competency 1, 11–12, 19–20
  and advance directives 53–4, 60–1
  during labour 66–7
  information disclosure 19–20
  learning disability 41–3, 44, 97–8,
    100–1
  mental illness 38–41, 44–5
  persistent vegetative states 50–1
  pre-operative sedation 12, 14, 15
  see also informed consent

PCC *see* Professional Conduct Committee
(PCC) proceedings
persistent vegetative state
and consent to treatment withdrawal
50–1
and organ/tissue donation   57–8
withholding nutrition and hydration   12
personhood   130–1
physician-assisted suicide   47, 53, 61
placebos   97
plastic surgery, and resource rationing
119
Polkinghorne Committee   131–2
Pope Pius XII   49
portfolios   90
pre-implantation genetic diagnosis
(PIGD)   72–3
pregnancy
and caesarean section   66–7, 78
legal relationship between mother and
fetus   66
pre-implantation genetic diagnosis
(PIGD)   72–3, 132–4
pre-natal screening   67–8, 137
right to refuse treatment   13
underage pregnancies   30–1, 36
Pretty, Diane   125
professional competency
and clinical mistakes   90
health problems (doctors)   84, 89
and licence to practice   90
and revalidation   90
seeking informed consent   13, 15
see also misconduct
Professional Conduct Committee (PCC)
proceedings   84, 88
professional misconduct *see* misconduct
prognosis delivery
patient's right to refuse information
4–5, 6–7
withholding information from patients
3–6
proxy consent   12, 41

quality adjusted life years (QUALYs)
frameworks   114–15

rationing and resources   111–19
availability of treatments   4–5
concept of 'basic need'   114

and discrimination   118
implications of Human Rights
legislation   112–13
and individual responsibility   117
NHS decision-making systems   116
NHS duties and obligations   111–14
NHS legal position   112
principles of beneficence and
justice   113–14
QUALYs/SAVEs frameworks   114–15
systems in other countries   116–17
resuscitation guidelines   54
revalidation   90
right to refuse to receive information   4–5,
6–7
right to refuse treatment   13, 16
and advance directives   53–4
children   30–1
emergency caesarean sections   78
see also withholding treatment
Riverside Mental Health NHS Trust v Fox
(1993)   41

saved young life equivalents (SAVEs)   115
screening
criteria   133
of gamete donors   69–70
genetic   132–3
pre-natal   67–8
R v Secretary of State for Health, ex p Pfizer
Ltd (1999)   118
*Seeking patient's consent: the ethical
considerations* (GMC)   13
smoking, and healthcare rationing   117
somatic gene therapy   133–4
sports injuries, and healthcare
rationing   117
sterilisation   75–6, 78
and informed consent   12, 41–2
students, support services   82–3
suicide, assisted   53, 61
surrogacy   73–4
Surrogacy Arrangements Act 1985   73

transplantation   55–60
categories   55
cadaveric donors   58
children donors   57
and informed consent   12, 14, 44
legal position   59–60

transplantation (*continued*)
  living donors   12, 14, 44, 56–8
  neonatal donors   58–9
  organ 'opt out' donation schemes   59
  resource allocation and alcoholic liver
      disease   18
  xenotransplantation   55
treatment availability *see* rationing and
      resources
truth   2–3
  withholding information   3–5
  and omission   3
  see also breaking bad news
Tuskegee study   95–6

Unrelated Live Transplant Regulatory
      Authority   56
USA, healthcare systems   116–17

websites   141–4
  clinical trials   104
  complaints procedures   94
  conduct of research   96, 98
  genetic testing   137

informed consent   14
medical research on human organs/
      tissues   102
medical research involving children
      101
'problem doctors'   94
research ethics committee   105, 106
revalidation advice   90
xenotransplantation   55
whistleblowing   *91*, 92
withholding information   3–6, 137
withholding treatment
  neonates   49–50
  persistent vegetative states   12, 50–1
World Health Organization (WHO)
  on 'health'   113, 130
  on screening   133

xenotransplantation   55

Re Y (adult patient) (transplant: bone
      marrow) (1997)   57

Z & others v UK   126